Translation Theory for Literary Translators

B.J. Woodstein

ANTHEM PRESS

Anthem Press
An imprint of Wimbledon Publishing Company
www.anthempress.com

This edition first published in UK and USA 2024
by ANTHEM PRESS
75–76 Blackfriars Road, London SE1 8HA, UK
or PO Box 9779, London SW19 7ZG, UK
and
244 Madison Ave #116, New York, NY 10016, USA

© B.J. Woodstein 2024

The author asserts the moral right to be identified as the author of this work.

All rights reserved. Without limiting the rights under copyright reserved above, no part of this publication may be reproduced, stored or introduced into a retrieval system, or transmitted, in any form or by any means (electronic, mechanical, photocopying, recording or otherwise), without the prior written permission of both the copyright owner and the above publisher of this book.

British Library Cataloguing-in-Publication Data
A catalogue record for this book is available from the British Library.

Library of Congress Cataloging-in-Publication Data
A catalog record for this book has been requested.
2024931648

ISBN-13: 978-1-83999-207-0 (Pbk)
ISBN-10: 1-83999-207-7 (Pbk)

This title is also available as an e-book.

For Fi, Esther and Tovah, as ever.

CONTENTS

Acknowledgements		vii
1.	Introduction	1
2.	Definitions	9
3.	Betwixt	19
4.	Identity	35
5.	Power	41
6.	Ethics	51
7.	Conclusion	69
Bibliography		71

ACKNOWLEDGEMENTS

I wish to thank the translation students I taught during my years at the University of East Anglia in England. The discussions we had and the questions and perspectives the students brought to class helped me expand my own views on the links between translation theory and translation practice.

In addition, I am grateful to the translators who answered my questions, on social media or in person, about their approaches, particularly in regard to ethics.

I must express my thanks to the peer reviewers, who made this work better with their suggestions, and also to the staff at Anthem, for another fruitful collaboration.

The authors, editors and literary agents I have worked with on translations have also influenced my thinking about what it means to translate, so I thank all of them for their contributions.

And, as always, I offer all my gratitude and appreciation to my wife, Fi, and our children, Esther and Tovah, for the joy and love they bring to my life every day. I never forget how lucky I am.

Chapter 1
INTRODUCTION

Translation theory for literary translators sounds like a dry subject. Indeed, many eyes glazed over when I mentioned my excitement about writing this book. However, I find that time spent discussing theoretical approaches to literary translation is both fascinating and fruitful and I hope to convince you of this too.

Part of the impetus for this book was that I often had students, whether at BA or MA level, who were curious about translation and were even considering being translators but who were scared of theory or uninterested in theoretical ideas. To them, being a translator just meant knowing their source and target languages well and having excellent writing and editing skills. They felt that theory was complicated and disconnected from their work as translators. They would dutifully read the texts I assigned, but sometimes found them challenging or said they thought theory was irrelevant. The academy was not the real world, they said, and they did not see why they should read work by people who had not necessarily worked as translators themselves. Of course, it is true that a university campus is not exactly the real world, but it is part of it, and personally, I disagreed with them about theory not having any practical value or application. As a translator myself, I do not consciously think of theory as I translate but the ideas are always present and I ponder them as I analyse texts. I love to read other people's discussions about what translation is, what it can do and how it might work, and I am inspired by this as I translate. As a teacher, I wanted to encourage my students to have a broad range of tools and concepts in their translatorial toolbox, and I think theory is an obvious and important tool.

But it is important to note that I do not believe theoretical ideas are simply applied while someone translates. Sure, it might happen that someone gets stuck on a thorny translatorial problem and remembers a strategy that they read about. More often, however, theoretical concepts stimulate thoughts and offer options and approaches. In my 20-plus years as a translator, I have not often thought, 'I read theory A that said I should do this, so I'll do it as I translate'. I actually think, 'I read theory A that said this and theory B that said that, and I like this aspect of A and that aspect of B, and yet my text is different and I feel it needs another approach. What can I take from those scholarly ideas to employ in my task today? What would make this translation a success, whatever success means for this particular work? And how does my actual work as a translator build on or challenge those theories I've read?'

Once I began explaining my process in this way to the students, they became much more open to translation theory. They read and debated the works, and they started sharing how their translation tasks helped them understand the theory in a new way. In other words, it became a circular give-and-take situation; translation theory stimulated their work, which stimulated their understanding of theory, which helped them develop theories of their own, which helped them think differently about their work, which … you get the point.

1.1 Theory

The obvious place to start here is to discuss what theory is generally and what translation theory is more specifically. There are multiple definitions for the word 'theory', so I think a dictionary is worth consulting. The Oxford English Dictionary initially offers '[t]he conceptual basis of a subject or area of study. Contrasted with *practice*' (OED, 'theory', n.p., italics original). Also, theory is '[a]bstract knowledge or principles, as opposed to practical experience or activity' (ibid.). Both these definitions emphasise the idea that theory is, well, theoretical; in other words, they suggest that theories are ideas or concepts, but are not the same as practical knowledge. While I am reluctant to argue with the august OED and I am very aware that some people do use theory in opposition to practice, I would prefer for us to see them as more linked than that, rather than as a strict dichotomy. Surely theory could describe what is done or what could be done, and it could in turn inform what happens, rather than being treated as if it were separate, and should remain thus.

But feel free to disagree with me, as others certainly suggest that the application of theory to practice, or the reverse, is not necessarily that simple or useful. Jean Boase-Beier notes, 'A theory is a partial description (mental or perhaps written down) of a segment of perceived reality, and so the attempt to apply it to any new situation has to be approached with extreme caution' (2010, p. 26). Caution, yes, and not all theories work in all situations, but I would argue that just talking theoretically about a field, such as translation, without considering and trying to see how the ideas apply to the actual practice of it may be interesting but not always relevant. Despite warning us about the danger of applying theory in an 'encompassing, simplistic' way (2010, p. 28), a danger I agree with, because it implies a lack of conscious thought regarding what one is doing and what context one is working in, Boase-Beier goes on to tentatively suggest application, by writing that 'theories are partial, descriptive, and represent different ways of seeing, [so] they should enable us to free ourselves from naïve conceptions of what translation is. And because they are explanatory they become part of the way we approach the world in a very practical sense. They may not dictate practice, but they will certainly influence it' (2010, p. 27).

Not all theories can or should be applied – theories, of course, can be purely theoretical, or they can be misguided or simply wrong, but they can be views of something, as Boase-Beier says (2010, p. 19), and they can describe, predict, suggest and perhaps even prescribe. Boase-Beier confirms that '[t]heory [...] can give us the confidence to try out other methods, explore other types of equivalence, or question degrees of closeness' (2010, p. 25).

If theory is a view or a description, then what is it specifically in terms of translation? Referring to the OED again, it defines 'literary theory' as 'the field of study concerned with inquiry into the evaluation, analysis, and understanding of literary works and (now also) other texts [...] often incorporating concepts from other disciplines, such as philosophy, politics, or sociology' (OED, 'literary theory,' n.p.). Similarly, 'translation theory' is defined as 'the theoretical study of translation, often incorporating concepts from disciplines such as linguistics, philosophy, psychology, and the social sciences' (OED, 'translation theory,' n.p.). It is interesting – and not surprising to those of us who work with literature and/or who are translators – that the definitions both emphasise interdisciplinarity. Theory, the OED seems to be saying, is a way of analysing and understanding texts and the practice of working on those texts, from a variety of different angles, some more language focused, others broader and more culture based and still others from different fields altogether. We should be promiscuous in our attempt to comprehend what exactly we are doing as translators.

Boase-Beier contends that within the field of translation studies, theory is, or should be, 'essentially descriptive' (2010, p. 27); there is even a whole area within the field called Descriptive Translation Studies. She emphasises again her belief that theory should not be applied: 'I am arguing against the naïve, unconsidered application of theory and even against any direct application of translation theory to the act of translation. Such theories are not meant to be sets of instructions and they serve translators, including the best poet-translators, badly when so used. Let us instead take on peripheral theories: of the text, the context, the reader, the effects of history, the nature of literature. They are more interesting, more useful, and far less dangerous' (2010, p. 36). But, as is probably clear, I do not agree – I think theories are tools and translators, especially as they develop, use their knowledge, including tools, in a way that I doubt is 'naïve' or 'unconsidered'. Sometimes the tools are mainly kept in the conceptual toolbox and form the basis of interesting thoughts or discussions. But sometimes an academic or a translator or a translator-scholar might suggest a strategy or a way of looking at a text that can directly be applicable to a different situation. Why is it 'dangerous' to apply it then?

Andrew Wilson writes

> The thing to remember is that translation theory is part of the wider field of translation studies, a vast and eclectic area of scholarship that draws from a wide variety of disciplines and from researchers in many countries. The best of it makes you think again about texts you thoughts you knew, as the translator not only becomes 'visible' but is subjected to the equivalent of a full MRI scan. Gender, politics, and ideology receive a much-needed airing, providing fuel for passionate polemical battles. (2009, p. 177)

This sounds so exciting – why would we not want to think about these topics, in relation to who we are and what we do and our place in the world?

Pilar Ordóñez López and Rosa Agost write that 'theoretical reflection contributes to translation practice' (2022, p. 159). They refer to studies that suggest that theory does not necessarily impact people's translation practice or that there is no connection (2022, p. 159). But besides those studies not providing the full picture, the obvious question is: why not? Why could or should translation theory not impact how people think about and carry out translation? Also, as implied already here, the practice of translation should impact how people understand, write about and develop translation theory; in other words, there could be a companion book to this one entitled *Translation Practice for the Translation Theorist*. Of course, there are many fields with a divide between theory/criticism and practice; for example, how many film critics write or produce or star in films? But this has always puzzled me. I think the influence and interaction between theory and practice should ideally, though not always, go in both directions.

So one obvious point is whether budding translators are taught about theory. Certainly, at both the university where I got my PhD in translation studies and the university where I taught for many years, students explored both translation theory and translation practice, although it was sometimes the case that there was a clear divide, in that the translation theory modules did not always include translation practice and the more supposedly 'creative' modules did not always insist on students reading the theoretical texts.

In the modules I taught, for both undergraduates and postgraduates, I insisted that our syllabus be creative-critical, which meant that each week we read and discussed theory, wrote our own responses to these ideas and came up with our own theoretical approaches, reviewed translated texts, translated work ourselves and tried to see connections between how both we and other people translated and the theoretical ideas about translation. Their assessments likewise combined their own work as translators with an analysis of translation theory. Many students appreciated this, while others decidedly did not, and would have preferred an either/or approach to theory and translation work.

Ordóñez López and Agost explored the training of translators in Spain and found that translation degrees there are 'practice-oriented' and yet that

> contrary to the findings of other scholars [...] our studies reveal that students do not draw a clear distinction between theory and practice and that they are less averse to theory than previously assumed. In light of these results, it could be deduced that, from the students' point of view, translation theory plays (or could play) an important role in their training as future translators. (2022, p. 160)

A follow-up question is how translation is taught as a subject in various universities. If translation theory is kept as a separate course/module, then it will look like there is a divide between theory and practice. But if it is integrated into other courses, then this will show students that there is a clear connection, as I tried to provide in the classes I taught.

Ordóñez López and Agost write that students find that the main issues with translation theory are 'density and/or volume of teaching materials' (2022, p. 163). In regard to density, perhaps as with literary theory and indeed theoretical concepts from other fields, this is partly a matter of accepting that theory can sometimes be hard and that effort has to be put into understanding it, and partly an issue of how theory is offered to beginning (or experienced) translators and how it is taught. As for volume, this is up to individual teachers – or those who are studying on their own – to decide, in regard to how much to assign or read at any given point, and how to combine it with practice.

Interestingly, in some circumstances, practising translators are educated in translation theory. Riikka Halme-Berneking writes that bible translators in Angola are given training, which, she claims, results in 'high-quality translations' (2019, p. 278). This situation is somewhat different in that the translators are arguably somewhat biased in their choice of work. (The Angolan government even employs translators from the Bible Society now for official documents (Halme-Berneking 2019, p. 282) and while this is not the space to discuss this issue, one wonders what impact this might have on the translation of these documents.) Further research would be needed to explore whether knowledge of theory really does increase the quality of the translated products.

In short, Ordóñez López and Agost found in their analysis of translation theory and students that the students felt that learning theory was 'essential' and that it helped them gain new skills (2022, p. 165). They conclude that they 'consider it essential for university students to acquire knowledge about the theoretical foundations of their field of study' (2022, p. 174). The findings of such a study might be different for more experienced translators. As we progress in a field, we might feel (rightly or wrongly) that we know an awful lot about it and do not need to study it as much, or we might get set in our ways and believe that we know how to translate and do not require input from some scholar who might be long dead or from a very different context. Personally, I find it inspiring to continue to read theory and I get new ideas and methodological ideas from it; I also enjoy the occasional metaphorical slap in the face, when someone's perspective challenges what I thought I knew and forces me to rethink my thoughts or actions. If theory 'is simply a way of looking at the world' (Boase-Beier 2010, p. 26), we can all do with more ways of understanding the world, no matter what our field.

Theory, I would suggest, should not be viewed as limiting or as something a translator must rigidly follow. Rather, theoretical ideas about translation vary; they can be intriguing, ridiculous, stimulating, confusing, helpful, useless and all sorts of other adjectives, or a combination of them. As translators, I hope we can enjoy reading translation theory and we can consider whether a given theory or group of ideas helps us with our practice. In turn, our work as translators may provide the foundation for scholars – who may, in fact, be us, the practising translators ourselves – to describe in future theoretical work.

1.2 This Book

I have tried to make my case that translation theory is useful for practitioners, and I hope the rest of this book will support that. It is important to note that this short book is not a history of translation, a summary of translation theories and their development, or an anthology of translation theory. There are already books out there that do that sort of work (e.g. Pym 2009 or Venuti 2004), although it is fair to critique some of those books and to try to make up for their lack. For example, Douglas Robinson edited a work entitled *Western Translation Theory from Herodotus to Nietzsche* (1997/2002). As the title suggests, all the authors/scholars included are from the West. And out of

90 authors, only a very few are female (Elizabeth Tudor, Margaret Tyler, Aphra Benn and a couple more). While undoubtedly Western men have had many interesting ideas, about translation and other topics, it is strangely limiting to only look at their work. For this reason, I am eager to explore a wider variety of thinkers on translation. For readers who wish to focus on Western men, I recommend Robinson's text, and I am sure you will find plenty of concepts in there that you could use to influence your work as a translator.

I personally have found it more useful to look both at the West and beyond. An interesting text by Judy Wakabayashi explores Japanese approaches and notes the need for 'alternative readings of translation' (2000, 259). As just one instance of a difference in views of translation, Wakabayashi writes

> One distinctive form that is indigenous to Japan and does not conform to Western expectations is the practice of *kambun kundoku*, which challenges such notions as the assumption that there are always separate source and target texts. Perhaps unique also is the practice of *rubi* glosses that give individual words two entirely different pronunciations and an extra layer of meaning. Japan also challenges the common perception that 'translationese' is undesirable […] translation was a way of enhancing the expressive capacities of the language. There has long been an acceptance of translations which are far removed in style, vocabulary and even structure from 'real' Japanese, and it could even be said that all modern written Japanese is to some extent translationese. (2000, p. 262, italics original)

I will return to differing definitions in the next section.

I had initially thought I would structure this book by historical period, starting with early views on translation, such as those of St Jerome or Dao An, and moving forward in time to range over Walter Benjamin, Gideon Toury, Luise von Flotow, Riitta Oittinen and so on, but ultimately, I realised that, again, there are books that provide this sort of overview. Instead, I take a more idiosyncratic approach. Thus, this book is a selection of ideas that translators can use in their practice. There are many theoretical approaches to translation and what I include here is inevitably limited. I confess that this is a biased selection of theories; I chose topics I have been teaching, reading or thinking a lot about in recent times, and I tried to let myself be moved by theories from different time periods, different cultures and languages, different genres and different approaches to translation.

The first section of this book explores what translation is and what translators do; as the quote from Wakabayashi reveals, translation is not a consistent concept across time or space; rather, it shifts and can at times seem amorphous.

Next, I analyse the key terms of fidelity, equivalence, distance and visibility, which frequently appear in translation studies. The following section looks at the ways that translation can complicate and shape identity, and then I explore power, which affects what is translated, by whom and how. The final section is on ethics, which brings many of the subjects together and which perhaps can be said to underpin the work that translators – and scholars – do. Please note that here I focus on literary translation, as a short book cannot do justice to all types of translation.

In sum, in this book, I offer a few examples of theoretical concepts and discussions and suggest ways that translators can engage with them. This is not a comprehensive anthology of translation theory, nor an analysis of every theoretical approach or idea. But I hope it will give you something to think about, whether you are a new or experienced translator and/or translation studies scholar.

Chapter 2

DEFINITIONS

While it may seem obvious what translation is and what translators do, the concept of translation varies depending on when and where the term is being used and is affected by culture, history and politics.

2.1 Translation

Any type of communication can require different forms of translation; speaking or writing could be called translation, as we have to express our internal thoughts in an external format, in a type of language that is different from the language in our heads, because the latter is our own idiolect. Salah Basalamah refers to all the different types of translation and writes about 'the broad distinction between translation in its traditional textual/verbal "narrow sense" including subtitling and interpretation, and translation in its broader sense which involves the mediation of diffuse symbols, experiences, narratives and linguistic signs of varying lengths across modalities (words into image, lived experience into words), levels and varieties of language (Standard Written Arabic and spoken Egyptian, for example), and cultural spaces, the latter without necessarily crossing a language boundary.' (2019, p. 184) That is, we are all translating all the time, from thoughts into words, and between dialects and registers and modes and media. However, for the sake of space, I want to focus on this 'narrow' view of translation, that is the textual one.

The Oxford English Dictionary offers several definitions of the term 'translation'. One is '[t]he action or process of translating a word, a work, etc., from one language into another' while another is '[a] version of a word, a work, etc., in a different language' (OED, 'translation', n.p.). In other words, there is the actual process of translating or the outcome of that process; Basil Hatim and Jeremy Munday ask whether translation is a process or a product (2004, pp. 3 and 6), while the OED differentiates between the two ideas, rightfully perhaps, because the word can, in English, cover both, even if we see a clear difference between process and product.

The OED definition does not specify whether the word or work to be translated can only be written, or whether oral texts count too; today, oral translation is often technically referred to as interpretation, whereas in casual conversation, I have found that most people outside of the field do not differentiate between translation and interpretation and either use them interchangeably or use one term to cover both written and oral works. Interpretation is a necessary activity in many contexts, such as at a doctor's office, in politics, or in religious situations. For the latter, Halme-Berneking notes that in Angola, preachers have their sermons simultaneously interpreted between Portuguese and Angolan (2019, p. 275). In this book, I am primarily referring to written translation, but many of the theoretical concepts can apply to the work of interpreters or translocators as well. When it comes to written translation, Roman Jakobson defined three types: 'intralingual, interlingual and intersemiotic', where intralingual is 'rewording' in the same language, interlingual, or 'translation proper' is between languages, and intersemiotic, or 'transmutation' is 'an interpretation of verbal signs by means of signs of nonverbal sign systems' (1959, p. 139). This book focuses on the interlingual.

All these give us a clear indication that translation is about the movement of a word, phrase or entire text from one language or format to another, but it does not go far enough. For one thing, it does not explore why someone would want or need to translate; to me, the simplest answer is to communicate.

Rita Kothari and Krupa Shah point out the challenge of defining translation in certain milieus

> [...] what is translation in the Indian context? Does it have to be linguistic in nature? Does it need to refer to written texts only? Does 'it' need to be called 'translation' or is it an unstable and hybrid category that has increasingly begun to get stable in a more self-conscious and academic understanding of translation? Does criss-crossing of languages often captured in misleadingly transactional terms such as 'borrowing' and 'loan words' not constitute translation? Do vocabularies from diverse regions not constitute what comes to be claimed as 'purely' indigenous languages, hinting at yet other processes of translation at work? To ask such questions is to remind ourselves not to assume what is perhaps best not assumed – the absence of a presence called 'translation.' (2019, p. 131)

They also note the variety of words used in India to describe translation and, as translators well know, different words have different associations. Kothari and Shah mention that translation was once seen as 'the rendering or the transference' but the influence of colonisers impacted the situation so that 'the term anuvad which in ancient texts occurs in the sense of "repeating, to follow" and "to say after," came to be an equivalent of "translation" in the sense of transference' (2019, p. 140). This is just one example of different words and understandings for translation, or a 'plurality of connotations' (2019, p. 146), as they phrase it.

G. Gopinathan writes extensively about what he terms transcreation in India. He says that 'creative translation was considered the proper mode of translating ancient Indian classics' (2000, p. 170), which implies that there are different types of translation for different types of texts. Gopinathan notes that transcreation is an interpretation, an aesthetic activity, which is not how all view translation as a whole, or even all literary translation, although he argues that '[t]*ranscreation is a living tradition with many possibilities for universal application*' (2000, p. 172, italics original). He says that to carry transcreation out, '*Transcreator enters into the soul of the original author.*' (2000, p. 171, italics original). He also explains that '[l]iterary translation in India was never considered something different in kind from creative activity' (2000, p. 165). Not everyone views literary translation as creative work – consider the fact that it is still relatively unusual for translators to be listed on the covers of books, as equal to the original authors, which is something that is only recently happening more, and only in some countries. And even if the creative nature of translation were acknowledged, it is an interesting question to ponder whether translation needs more than general literary theories, that is whether translation theory itself is required.

At any rate, not all theorists accept the idea of translation being a creative activity and the concept of transcreation does not exist everywhere. Wakabayashi highlights how varied and culturally shaped our views of translation are when she writes

> Expectations in Asia of what constitutes 'translation' have varied over time and space, from the highly interlinear [as in Japan] [...] to 'transcreation' (India), from intralingual translations [...] to intersemiotic translations. The values attached to different practices have also varied cross-culturally – for example, free translation has generally been regarded in a negative light in Japan, unlike in India. (2001, p. 25)

Meanwhile, Said Faiq writes that in the Arab tradition, there are three forms of translation, but a version of transcreation is not among them

1. Literal translation [...] [where] translators considered each source language word and its meaning and then used an approximately similar Arabic word. Often this meant that they transliterated

technical terms, and the structures and style of the Arabic translations were stilted and odd [...].
2. Semantic translation. Translators [...] adopted and practiced a semantic strategic which involved reading the original, processing it, and trying to find semantically equivalent structures in Arabic, regardless of structure or lexical equivalence. Most translations produced according to this strategy did not require any revision or rewriting.
3. Gist translation [...] which involved summary rather than full translation. This translation strategy came to be used because the need for more translation of Greek and other works diminished when Arab scholars started writing and publishing their own research. (2000, p. 86)

Although these three activities are quite obviously different in both approach and aim – the intention being, respectively, to summarise ideas, show what the original said or adapt the meaning of the text to the target language – they all were and perhaps are, it seems, considered legitimate forms of translations.

Halme-Berneking notes that in Angola, oral translation is key, particularly in religious situations, and the context influences the translatorial choices that are made: '[o]ral translation practiced at church services or in political speeches and meetings is generally more idiomatic and meaning-based, often even tending toward paraphrase' (2019, p. 283). Halme-Berneking goes on to note that, on the other hand, in Angola, '[w]ritten translation is often expected to be more literal, word-for-word translation, essentially replacing words of one language with words of another language, and paying less attention to the overall meaning of the text or to the different morpho-syntactic structures and idiomatic expressions of each language' (2019, p. 283). This is not necessarily how written translation is viewed in European countries.

In Israel too, the religious context affects how people understand what translation is and what a translator does. Nitsa Ben-Ari and Shaul Levin explain that

> The term turgeman or meturgeman (derived from the semitic root trgm meaning translate/interpret), used to describe the translator or interpreter, had actually at various periods denoted a person – always a man – tasked with reading the translation of the Torah in the course of its ritual reading at the synagogue; a person tasked with pronouncing the sage's words addressed to the public and at times explaining them;

and a so-called speech-mediator, especially between God and man.[...] Translation has been instilled as a legitimate socio-cultural necessity, given place and role in society, and, over time, institutionalized. (2019, p. 196)

They add that the use of a translator was pragmatic because a translator was needed to help provide and even explain the word of God to people attending synagogue. Ben-Ari and Levin refer to a hierarchy in traditional Israeli (or, perhaps it is better to say, Jewish) perspectives: a 'translation was to be permitted only as an act of explanation or interpretation, as commentary to the original which it must accompany. The translated text, in itself, holds no ritualistic value' (2019, p. 197). In those contexts, translation was for religious purposes and was practical; it could be argued that it was both a way of sharing ideas and also a method of controlling people. This is not the whole picture for modern Israel, of course (consider the influential theoretical work on translation carried out there by, among others, Gideon Toury and Miriam Shlesinger), and could be said to describe the view on translation in other religious contexts, such as Angola.

In opposition to this, translation is seen as much more than pragmatic or as a form of paraphrase in other places. For instance, Simos Grammenidis and Giorgios Floros note that in the Greek-speaking countries (chiefly Greece and Cyprus), translators are 'thought of as interpreting agents, creators and mediators between two worlds' (2019, p. 333). This description places a high level of agency on the translator, suggesting a certain amount of power and importance, which contrasts with some people's beliefs that a translator is merely someone who reads in one language and then types the supposedly equivalent words in another language; this is the sort of view that leads some people to say, 'Why do you need translators when you have Google translate?' The Greek view suggests that translators are creative, which is how you would describe an artist; Gopinathan describes a similar view in India, where '[l]iterary translation [...] was never considered something different in kind from creative activity' (2000, p. 165). Gopinathan specifies literary translation, which implies that more technical forms of translation – perhaps including works such as users' manuals, cookbooks, pharmaceutical documentation, legal texts and so forth – are not creative, and this is a debatable point, but nonetheless, the Greek and Indian views, which are far from the only ones to see translation as creative, may make us consider the idea that a translator is an author, making artistic decisions about a text.

Both the Israeli and the Greek perspectives on translation reference mediation. In the case of the former, the mediation is between 'God and man' (Ben-Ari and Levin 2019, p. 196), and thus is of importance for one's soul, while in the latter description, it is about facilitating communication between two people or groups. With this in mind, one could argue that translators bring people together and perhaps can even prevent or smooth over problems. Truly, that is a powerful role.

Related to this, translation is situational and may be required to engage with or combat even larger issues than some of the religious examples mentioned. Basalamah quotes Samah Selim, who 'suggests that there are two types of militant translations: "crisis translation" and "deep translation"' (2019, p. 184). Selim goes on to explain that

> 'crisis translation' is done in the urgency of the moment, when a specific event or series of events require immediate dissemination to the outside world, on the order of 'this is happening now!' while 'deep translation' 'moves beyond image and spectacle, with the intention of building international solidarity networks that are nonetheless firmly rooted in the granular struggles of a particular place.[...] These kinds of targeted translation efforts are the building blocks of sustained political information campaigns and collaborations.' (2019, p. 185)

Both require significant knowledge, potentially even participation in the events taking place and perhaps membership in a particular community. Clearly, this sort of translation is not always relevant, as, thankfully, not all humans are always in crisis and we are not always in a struggle of the type that Selim and Basalamah discuss. But there will be times when such revolutionary, involved translation is required.

Many seem to agree with Marina Schwimmer that 'translation is perhaps best understood as an accumulation of meanings' (2017, p. 58), but which meanings and how they are accumulated and how you as a translator need to accumulate them in your new text are not always clear. You as a translator might want to read these and other ideas and try to determine where you situate yourself on the broad spectrum of views of translation.

But if scholars and translators cannot agree on what translation is, then how do we know what we as translators should be doing?

2.2 What a Translator Needs to Be

Together, some of these conceptions of translation begin to help us shape an idea of who and what a translator should be. Schwimmer states that

> practitioners are neither executants nor experts who resolve predetermined problems, but rather [...] they are constantly committed

to improvisation whenever they seek creative and spontaneous solutions for each situation. In order not to fall into habits or routines, they must reflect on their work during the action and after the action and constantly build on their experience. (2017, p. 54)

Translators, then, are expected to reflect on the text we are translating, on the experience of translating and on the aftermath of each task. One could argue that part of the reflection is reading and thinking about theory and trying to gain new ideas from others who translate and/or work on translation.

If a translator is to mediate between cultures and languages, we might expect a translator to be someone who is very familiar with both (or all) groups concerned and who has a sense of their needs and perspectives. Likewise, seeing translation as a creative task indicates that a translator must be someone who is talented with words. It could be argued that they have to be equal in talent to the original author, in order to recreate that author's text in a new form and language. Author and translator Vladimir Nabokov actually recommended the following skills and attributes for a translator: 'as much talent, or at least the same kind of talent, as the author he chooses'; thorough knowledge of 'the two nations and the two languages involved' and of 'all details relating to his author's manner and methods; also, with the social background of words, their fashions, history and period associations'; 'the gift of mimicry' and the ability to 'act, as it were, the real author's part by impersonating his tricks of demeanor and speech, his ways and his mind, with the utmost degree of verisimilitude' (1941, n.p.). Nabokov clearly has very high expectations (and also the apparent opinion that translators are only male), and it is not always possible for every translator to have each of those particular traits for every single job; however, it is certainly worth aiming for (cf. Gopinathan 2000, p. 166). To sum up these ideas: a translator should be an expert on the author, the languages and the cultures, and also be a talented writer in their own right.

As Nabokov and Gopinathan suggest and as Basalamah nicely sums up (2019, p. 178), a translator is expected to accomplish so much – not just to bring across the ideas in a general sense, but also to explicate them, and to benefit people by doing so – that it is perhaps unsurprising that theorists have begun to place potentially unreachable demands on translators and to have unrealistic expectations about who can be a translator. When I visit primary and secondary schools to talk about being a translator, I often discuss the importance of strong language skills and a detail-oriented approach to reading, analysing, writing and editing, but I try not to scare off budding translators by suggesting that they must know everything about the source and target cultures and literatures and that they must work for the benefit of authors, readers and groups of people as a whole. I emphasise that you learn and improve with each translation you carry out. If we required huge swathes of knowledge that, arguably, most writers and scholars do not possess, no one would dare to try to translate.

Another approach is to say that translation is impossible. Schwimmer suggests that perhaps we should give up on the idea of a good translation and being a perfect translator; if we accept failure/lack from the start, or at least accept that perfection is impossible (as it is in all areas of life), we could 'grieve' this impossibility (2017, p. 57) and then move on with the task of translating, producing an end product of some kind.

To close this section, I want to refer to metaphors of translation and metaphors for translators as people and for the work we do. Nabokov's comments argued that a translator should be able to 'impersonate' an author (1941, n.p.). This is a fascinating word choice, because it relates to acting and performing, and perhaps carries with it a whiff of falsity (an impersonator is, after all, a fraud). Using another job or concept as a way of understanding what a translator is and does is common in translation theory. A few examples, other than Nabokov's impersonator and related ideas of ventriloquism and acting, include the translator as a clockmaker, musician, adoptive parent, tailor, handmaiden/servant, horticulturist, actor, wine-maker, traitor, anthropologist, driver or someone who transports others, ghost, painter, printmaker, chess-player, captain or sailor, conductor or tightrope-walker (see, e.g. Chaffee 2016, n.p. or St. André 2011, pp. 84–7). It is perhaps not surprising that many of these metaphors highlight artistry and/or movement. But some metaphors are not positive in their connotations. As Polly Barton points out, there is often a belief (usually among non-translators) that translation is an automated, easy task. She writes that when she is talking to others who do not translate

> I start to build up a picture of translation as they conceptualize it.[...] In this representation of it, translation is akin to an elaborate autocorrect function [...] to move a text between two languages, all I have to do is switch the Japanese words over to their relevant English correlates, and then maybe fiddle about with the order a little, in order to yield the correct translation as the sentence level. (2021, p. 163)

So a translator is the autocorrect feature on a phone or computer. As artificial intelligence becomes more developed and more widely available in the world of translation, some worry that this automation will become more common; space precludes me from discussing this more, but automated motion from one is another intriguing, and potentially concerning, metaphor to ponder.

2.3 From Theory to Practice

As many of the quotes and concepts referred to above reveal, translators do not translate in a vacuum; we are influenced by the time and place where we live and work and by our culture's perspective on translation. If, for instance, we live somewhere that feels translation should be a paraphrase in order to best get across the purported word and message of a god or a religious leader, then we will probably feel we can take more liberties with a text and will be less focused on the individual words than on the overarching message. If we live in a culture that perceives translators as creative artists who must be knowledgeable about literature and skilful at writing, we will be trained as translators differently, will work differently and will view ourselves in another way than if we live in a time and place that considers us to be servants. Besides the context in which we work, we are also influenced by issues such as the translator education we have had (if any), the type of text we are translating, the languages we are working with, the client we are working for, our contact with other translators and more. Although we cannot escape the influence of all these things, we have the right and even the responsibility to think for ourselves and to use our understanding of translation as a field to determine how we work. So, what does translation mean in your culture(s)? What are translators expected to be and to do? What do you think about those skills, requirements and notions? What sort of translator do you want to be and what sort do you think you have the aptitude to be? What is your aim when translating and how does it change depending on circumstances? What approaches do you take when translating a given type of text? Why do you translate?

Chapter 3
BETWIXT

Translation is, quite obviously, in between. It is in between languages, cultures, people and time periods, among other things. A number of different theoretical concepts and discussions regarding translation explore this in-betweenness, from a variety of angles, that is fidelity, equivalence, domestication/foreignization (in other words, distance) and visibility. Fidelity and equivalence are considered so essential to the work of translators that they are even codified in a number of translators' association's guidelines and codes of conduct, although some scholars suggest that they do not belong there or perhaps should be considered ethical matters (Bennett 2021, p. 46). Some of the relevant questions are as follows: How 'faithful' must a translator be and to whom or what? How equivalent must the source and target texts be and what does equivalence even mean in this context? Should a translator bring the text to the reader or encourage the reader to approach the text? How visible should the translator be and who is responsible for the visibility? All of these issues are on a continuum, although some translators and scholars insist that one binary position is more correct than another.

In this section, I explore the betwixt nature of translation. I also adapt an idea from the world of sexology to suggest that being a little less 'vanilla' in our approach may be a way forward and could help us get out of the position where we are 'stuck between a rock and a hard place', and instead into one in which we may be comfortable between the two, with a hand resting on either side. That is, I believe that allowing ourselves to slide along the continuum works better than trying to rigidly choose one side, even if having a more black-and-white/right-and-wrong approach might seem easier and more appealing, because it implies that all a translator needs to do is to figure out the correct option.

3.1 Fidelity

One of the most common concepts in translation theory is fidelity or faithfulness. The Oxford English Dictionary offers an initial definition: 'Of a person or animal (esp. a dog): constant in allegiance or affection; loyal, true *to* (one's friend, master, etc.).' and 'Of a partner in a marriage or other relationship: sexually loyal to the other partner; not adulterous.', among other definitions (OED, n.d., 'faithful', italics original). The reference to 'dog' makes me think of a dogsbody, which takes us to servitude (one of our metaphors). Indeed, terms that appear frequently in the OED list of meanings for 'faithful' include 'loyal', 'true' and 'reliable', with other synonyms and related terms featuring as well. To be faithful is to be loyal, but when I look up 'loyal', the definitions contain the words 'faithful' and 'true', which might seem to be something of a tautology.

On a cursory internet search, I find that fidelity means staying close to the source text. For instance, one website says '[f]aithfulness in translation defines how a translated document follows the source and how much it keeps the original message' (TranslateDay 2021, n.p.). This is vague because it refers to the 'message' but then later in the same document focuses on being faithful to 'style', 'terms', '[v]ocabulary, grammar, syntax and structure of the original language', 'reserving untranslated idioms, rhetorical devices and diction' (I think they mean 'preserving' rather than 'reserving') and 'audience', among other ideas (ibid.). Obviously, this is just one blog post by one translation company, which would certainly have a stake in how translators work and how clients think about the work, but I think it is indicative of the confusion that exists.

If you know more than one language, you will immediately be aware that sticking closely to original words or idioms is generally not possible; even two closely related languages work differently and words have different connotations and uses. If you look beyond the specific words, which aspect of the text is a translator meant to focus their efforts on? Besides the words, there is the tone, the feeling, the style, the plot, the rhythm, the rhyming (if relevant), the images (again, if relevant), the audience, the message, the intention behind the writing/publishing of the text, the 'spirit' (a diffuse concept, certainly) or one of the other qualities a given text has. If a translator chooses one as the main priority, this may be to the detriment of another. Some even think that if you are too faithful, whatever that actually means, you might risk a text not looking or sounding appealing, or vice versa. As Mark Polizzotti writes, 'It was the seventeenth-century French critic Gilles Ménage who coined the term *les belles infidèles* (the beautiful, unfaithful ones), after a venerably sexist French adage likening translations to women, in that they can be comely or faithful but never both' (2018, p. 49, italics original). The misogyny inherent in this phrase is recognised today, but the idea nonetheless remains that a translation has to be faithful in order to be 'right' or, indeed, 'beautiful'.

Maria Tymoczko explains, in reference to challenging aspects of the text in particular, how 'the translator is faced with the dilemma of faithfulness: to be "faithful", such problematic factors must be transposed despite the difficulties they might cause to the sensibilities or cognitive framework of translator or audience; in obscuring or muting the cultural disjunctions, the translator ceases to be "faithful" to the source text' (1999, p. 21). Tymoczko argues that authors can be 'aggressive', as she phrases it, in their choices (1999, p. 21), but can a translator? Translators are generally expected to be more servile, which often seems to mean that translators feel more constricted and do not believe they can be as creative as a text may require, or 'aggressive' perhaps, as the original writer.

And yet, despite knowing the challenges inherent to fidelity, we translators are drawn to the concept and we sometimes even defend our work by commenting on its fidelity. For example, poet, translator and retired academic George Szirtes writes that he translated poems from Hungarian to English 'painstakingly, as faithfully as I could' (2009, n.p.). He adds

> *A faithful translation*: we think we know what we mean by the expression. It means not putting in too much that isn't there; trying to maintain a respectable degree of similarity of tone and form; and hoping that the impression made on the reader in the receiving language resembles, as closely as possible (as closely as you can judge) the impression made on the reader in the original language. (2009, n.p., italics original)

Szirtes concludes, 'As a translator I try to enter the spirit of the text (if I can locate it) then hope to travel through the English in a similar spirit. It is all travelling: travelling hopefully and never arriving.' (ibid.) This suggests that faithfulness is perhaps foremost in the spirit of the work and in the 'impression' a text makes on the audience. Helpfully, this moves the concept of fidelity away from individual words, which allows for more flexibility on the part of the translator.

Vinay Dharwadker suggests that a reader wants (or, I might add, that a reader believes they want) faithfulness while a translator works best when shifting away from fidelity

> A text's resistance to translatability [...] arises from the differences between language-systems as well as, among other things, from the conflict between author and translator [...] the relationship between translator and author is subject to two pairs of contradictory desires, with the pairs contradicting each other in turn. One coupling consists of the translator's desire to make a poem out of the translation, and the negation of this desire by the reader's conventionalized demand for

metaphrase or absolute literal fidelity to the original (without regard to its 'poetry'). The other coupling, with conflicts with the first, consists of the translator's desire to make out of the poetry of the original a poem of his or her own, and the negation of this desire by the obligation, conventionally enforced by readers, faithfully to make out of the intertextual encounter someone else's poem. (1999, p. 119)

I am not convinced that readers do want 'literal fidelity' or, rather, if they do, then perhaps they do not fully understand either translation or poetry. Still, there is a tension between desires in regard to who or what is faithful, and to whom or what they are faithful. Kruger and Crots suggest that translators are wary of making changes to texts, or being less than literal or faithful, when it comes to words or topics that are considered more challenging (2014, p. 177), perhaps as they are more likely to be criticised for taking liberties in such situations.

Maria Tymoczko and Edwin Gentzler write that translation

is not simply an act of faithful reproduction but, rather, a deliberate and conscious act of selection, assemblage, structuration, and fabrication – and even, in some cases, of falsification, refusal of information, counterfeiting, and the creation of secret codes. In these ways translators, as much as creative writers and politicians, participate in the powerful acts that create knowledge and shape culture. (2003, p. xxi)

In other words, perhaps translators can be 'aggressive', to use Tymoczko's aforementioned term, or can allow themselves the freedom to not be stringently loyal to the words, or even to other aspects of a text. Tymoczko and Gentzler even use language that seems antonymous to faithfulness, such as 'fabrication', 'falsification' and 'counterfeiting'. Perhaps by being false or disloyal in some ways, translators are in fact being faithful to the text as a whole and to the message and aims of it.

Christiane Nord has introduced the term 'loyalty' as a replacement concept. Here, the translator might focus on their duties towards people more than the text. She writes that translators 'have a special responsibility both with regard to their partners, i.e. the source-text author, the client or commissioner of the translation, and the target-text receivers, and towards themselves, precisely in those cases where there are differing views as to what a "good" translation is or should be. As an inter*personal* category referring to a social relationship between individuals who expect not to be betrayed in the process, loyalty may replace the traditional inter*textual* relationship of "fidelity", a concept that usually refers to a linguistic or stylistic similarity between the source and the target texts' (2007, p. 3, italics original).

This might lead us to question our own and others' motives when translating or reading a given text.

If we return to the OED definitions that started this section, there are a couple of other points of interest. One is the link to adultery, which is perceived as a negative concept; I will explore this more a little later. The other is the phrase 'in allegiance', tucked away in the first definition. I would suggest that in the context of translation, we often understand 'faithful' to be a rather strict concept, often relating to following what the source text says and trying to do or say the same in the target text; this leads to some of the prescriptive instructions that translators are offered at times in regard to how we should translate. However, the concept of being 'in allegiance' with the text might serve us better. Being 'in allegiance' might be defined as being loyal (Nord 2007) and faithful to someone or something, which would mean that we are back to the tautological issue we faced before, but perhaps we could consider it to mean that we are an 'ally' to a work. I might define this as wanting the best for the text, as helping and supporting the text (and, perhaps by association, the author). This does not mean having to agree with and exactly follow every word or concept in the text – harkening back to Tymoczko and Gentzler's idea that translators can be creative and sometimes even 'false' in their work – but it does mean uniting with it and promoting it to the best of your ability. Of course, in some cases, you might translate a text that you do not want to ally with; see the section on ethics. In sum, perhaps loyalty and allyship are more pertinent terms today.

3.2 Equivalence

For some people, fidelity and equivalence are interchangeable, but for other scholars and translators, they can be teased apart, because faithfulness might mean staying close to one or more aspects of a text, while equivalence implies ensuring that one or more parts of a work are the same in the source and the text. Both concern how literal or how free a translator can be. As Hatim and Munday write, 'The split between **form** and **content** is linked in many ways to the major polar split which has marked the history of western translation theory for two thousand years, between two ways of translating: "**literal**" and "**free**"' (2004, p. 11, emphasis original). They note that Cicero and St Jerome wrote about this, discussing having a word-for-word translation versus one that was more about the style and content. Other words are used to explore this same idea, namely the question of how creative translators can or should be when working.

Eugene Nida was a theorist who focused on bible translation, which could be viewed as a specific subset of translation, since one of the foremost goals of Christians, and those who translate Christian work, is to convert people to Christianity. Nida developed the terms formal equivalence and dynamic equivalence. Formal equivalence 'is basically source-oriented: that is, it is designed to reveal as much as possible of the form and content of the original message' (1964/2004, p. 161). Nida prescribes that a translator carrying out a translation that is formally equivalent would 'reproduce several formal elements, including: (1) grammatical units, (2) consistency in word usage, and (3) meanings in terms of the source text.' (ibid.) A few examples include 'translating nouns by nouns' and 'preserving all formal indicators', such as punctuation or line/paragraph breaks (ibid.). The point of this is to produce a text that 'aims at so-called concordance of terminology' (ibid.); the title of Nida's seminal work is 'Principles of Correspondence', and clearly 'correspondence', 'concordance' and 'equivalence' are all terms that suggest that there are one-to-one matches between words and language usage in the source language and in the target language. As the section above on fidelity mentioned, this is evidently not the case, even for tongues that are so similar that they might be considered dialects rather than separate languages. Schwimmer sums it up well

> Each culture develops its own ways of seeing, saying and feeling, and much of what goes on in a language cannot be exactly replicated in another. Interestingly, it is precisely this impossibility that enables the creation of new meanings: when confronted with the task of preserving the aesthetic dimension of a text, a translator has to be creative and adapt the language, which opens up a space for new concepts to emerge and for transformation to occur. (2017, p. 57)

A concentrated focus on linguistic or a broader formal equivalence does not allow for the opening up that Schwimmer seems to regard as a positive aspect of translation.

Nida's other approach is dynamic equivalence, which he says is 'directed, not so much toward the source message, as toward the receptor response' (1964/2004, p. 162), which is understandably relevant when it comes to bible translation, as the earlier example of Angola explained. He says the translation still 'must clearly reflect the meaning and intent of the source' (1964/2004, p. 163), but needs to be adjusted so it fits '(1) the receptor language and culture as a whole, (2) the context of the particular message, and (3) the receptor-language audience' (ibid.). For the first part of that sentence, it is worth pointing out that a translator is only one interpreter of a text, so may not understand the meaning of a section of the work or the work as a whole, nor can one person ever truly know the intentions behind someone's acts, whether they are in writing or otherwise. In other words, the idea of translation reflecting the meaning and intent exactly seems to me to be impossible, even if we translators strive for it. Schwimmer writes that translation is a balance 'between having to preserve the meaning of a source text while having to adapt it in order to take the target language's specificities into account' (2017, p. 51), which means that it is a creative task.

The concept of dynamic equivalence is potentially more flexible than formal equivalence because it is possible to push formal equivalence so far that the text becomes ridiculous. It may not, for instance, be the best choice to translate a noun with a noun because it could warp the target sentence into incomprehensibility. Nida notes '[a] translation which aims at dynamic equivalence inevitably involves a number of formal adjustments, for one cannot have his formal cake and eat it dynamically too' (1964/2004, p. 166). He suggests, however, that there are three main types of work that do not allow for a text to be both dynamically and formally equivalent: '(1) special literary forms [such as poetry], (2) semantically exocentric expressions [such as idioms], and (3) intraorganismic meanings [i.e. culturally-dependent expressions]' (ibid.).

Lawrence Venuti notes that terms such as formal equivalence and dynamic equivalence 'derive from traditional dichotomies between "sense-for-sense" and "word-for-word"' (2000/2004, p. 148), and he suggests, as do I, that theories such as Nida's do not raise 'fundamental doubts about the possibility of equivalence' (ibid.). I think that a given text may require shifts in approach, with a focus on the formal working better in some places, attention to the dynamic aspects more important elsewhere, and so on, but I also wonder whether equivalence is even something translators should be trying to reach. Is any sort of equivalence ever possible? Barton explores the concept of 'the correct translation', which seems to mean in part an equivalent work. She finds that the word 'correct' is often used in conversation with non-translators, and

> each time I will feel a sort of pang, which I don't quite know how to interpret. At times I wonder if it is a yearning for the days when I could still place trust in the meaning of those words, and use them with no critical awareness, no sense of suspicion towards the assumptions on which they rest. Or maybe it's closer to an imagined nostalgia for the world if it were really as my interlocutor believed: if there really were a singular, correct translation for each word, and translation operated on the word level, and the task of the translator were to reproduce the exact number of words that appeared in the original, and so on. I wouldn't want a world like that, but it would make things a lot more straightforward. (2021, p. 163)

Barton notes it would be more 'straightforward' if translators only had to reproduce a text exactly and offer an equivalent version in a new language but this is not what happens. As so many people seem to have the belief that translation is a matter of correspondence, to use Nida's term, it is often easy to criticise translators for their work. Barton describes a 'dog-eat-dog reality behind fluency', where 'language is not only a performance, but a performance where a single mistake can herald the end of you if you don't have the technique or the mental resilience that day to find your way around it' (2021, p. 252).

Gopinathan has a different perspective on equivalence than Nida. He writes, 'The nature of equivalence in transcreation will be cultural, aesthetic and communicative. Hence a holistic approach will be needed in evaluating translation equivalence in transcreation' (2000, p. 171). I would add that 'a holistic approach' seems appropriate both when translating (or transcreating, depending on the context and the preferred terminology) and when evaluating translations. The latter could perhaps avoid what Barton called the 'dog-eat-dog' world.

In short, equivalence means many different things, depending on text type, aim, translator and so forth, and even if equivalence were a well-defined concept, it is unfeasible – perhaps even to the point of ridiculousness – to suggest that a translator could make a text wholly equivalent to the original. Surely that would in fact be an exact copy, word-for-word, punctuation mark-for-punctuation mark, line break-for-line break and so on, of the original: that is, even down to the language. In other words, it would not be a translation at all. Different texts call for different approaches, but perhaps what translators might aim for in general is an equivalence of reading experience, so the text, to the best of their ability, uses similar language and style and has approximately the same message and impact.

3.3 Distance

How to ensure this similarity and how to bridge the distance between the author/text and the reader has long been a point of discussion in translation studies. Over two centuries ago, for example, Fredrich Schleiermacher wrote, 'Either the translator leaves the writer in peace as much as possible and moves the reader towards him; or he leaves the reader in peace as much as possible and moves the writer towards him' (1813/2004, p. 49). Leaving aside the presumed 'he', this sums up the alleged dichotomy; Schleiermacher uses 'either...or' – or, rather, his translator does. The question seems to be: how much work does the reader have to do? Or, put differently, should a translator simplify a text for the reader or should a reader be encouraged to make the effort to try to grasp a text in a form that is relatively close to its original?

Theo Hermans explains these two options in more detail. About the first one, which 'leaves the reader in peace', Hermans says it

> would have the translator write what the foreign author would have written had he not been foreign. But, Schleiermacher argues, if the author had grown up in our tongue, he would have been a different person entertaining different thoughts. This option assumes that the same thoughts can be thought in two different languages and that consequently thinking and language can exist separately. (2018, n.p.)

However, to leave 'the writer in peace' is

> equally impossible, but for a different reason. The translator can gain at best a partial, fragmentary understanding of the foreign author. With even the translator denied full access, there can be no question of the reader being transported to the author. The point at which author and reader meet can only be the translator. (ibid.)

Hermans concludes, 'It is therefore the translator who moves, taking the reader with him, and both firmly stay within the confines of their own tongue' (ibid.).

It is intriguing how much the idea of there being a bilateral approach has stayed with translation theorists. Venuti, for instance, developed Schleiermacher's ideas further, labelling them with the terms domestication and foreignization. Venuti does caution, however, that

> [a]ny significance assigned to the terms 'domestication' and 'foreignization' or 'fluency' and 'resistancy,' any application of them to a specific translation project, must be treated as culturally variable and historically contingent, dependent on acts of interpretation that are informed by archival research and textual analyses and, like every interpretation, are subject to challenge and revision on the basis of different critical methodologies and in response to developing cultural debates. (1995/2008, p. 19)

In other words, Venuti assigns names to Schleiermacher's approaches but warns that they should not be applied to a translation project without real thought and critique (which links back to Boase-Beier's urgent warnings), and he explains they can both be perceived as violent in their way (1995/2005, pp. 13–20), whether the violence is 'inherent in the translation process [...] [or] potential' (1995/2005, p. 15). Nonetheless, Venuti calls domestication 'ethnocentric' and foreignization 'ethnodeviant' (ibid.), and says 'I want to suggest that insofar as foreignizing translation seeks to restrain the ethnocentric violence of translation, it is highly desirable today.[...] Foreignizing translation in English can be a form of resistance against ethnocentrism and racism, cultural narcissism and imperialism, in the interests of democratic geopolitical relations' (1995/2005, p. 16). Venuti on the one hand advises against using these dichotomous approaches as strategies, but then specifically praises the potential effects of one of them (foreignization), encouraging translators to use it when translating to English; whether he views it as the right strategy for translations into other, less dominating languages is unclear from Venuti's work. Basalamah, referring to the translation of philosophy in particular to Arabic, uses the term 'acquisitive/perceptive translation [...] which consists of a more faithful transfer of the source text in its entire linguistic and formal granularity [...] a strategy that may be assimilated to the foreignizing strategy as found in Venuti' (2019, p. 189). So there is a potential implication that foreignizing may work when translating to Arabic, which is not as hegemonic as English, and also that it may be important for translating philosophy.

There are two key points here. The first is that there are many types of texts, assignments, clients or audiences that will force a choice of strategy. Basalamah's reference to philosophy showed that another example is in Iran, where the state mandates how domesticating or foreignizing a translation should be; as Omid Azadibougar and Esmaeil Haddadian-Moghaddam write, this means works are more likely to have to be domesticated there (2019, p. 160). In addition, if you are translating for people who are learning to read, whether they are children or adults, then foreignizing the text to further a political or cultural agenda may not serve your readers (although it could).

Second, a translator need not choose only between the two approaches, nor is it always the case that domestication is ethnocentric, and thus to be avoided; likewise foreignization is not always ethnodeviant and therefore to be favoured. One interesting aspect of making the reader do more work is that a translator may end up retaining untranslated words and concepts from the original. This could be because there are no existing translations or because the translator does not feel they have the time, the right or the ability to search for or create translations, or because retaining aspects of the source language is an elitist way of ensuring only certain target readers can access the translation, or as a way of educating/controlling the audience, or in order to preserve a specific culture or set of beliefs, or for any number of other reasons.

In other words, foreignization could expand the target language or culture or it could be an abuse of power over it.

In Angola, Halme-Berneking found that 'a number of newer or ad hoc loans appear in Portuguese and are essentially untranslated' (2019, pp. 278–80). Venuti notes that 'foreignizing translation can be useful in enriching the minority language and culture while submitting them to ongoing interrogation' (1995/2008, p. 20), but I think it is possible to label the situation in Angola postcolonialism. Instead of developing Umbundu, it appears that translators are importing untranslated terms from Portuguese and thereby bringing in the dominating, colonialising Portuguese culture and language.

Tymoczko suggests that foreignizing approaches such as '[t]he use of rare or untranslated words in translations and the inclusion of unfamiliar cultural material are not necessarily defects of translated texts [...] [t]he result is, however, that translations very often have a different lexical texture from unmarked prose in the receptor culture' (1999, p. 25). The question is, then, whether marked prose is productive. Marked prose also adds, as Tymoczko calls it, 'the problem of information load' and having to explain things to readers (1999, p. 30), or expecting readers to just understand. In a study I carried out many years ago, I explored translations from English to Swedish of idioms in children's books. I found that translators frequently did retain foreign idioms, literally translating them to the target language, sometimes adding in an explanation. My analysis suggested that this was an intriguing way of expanding the target language, because it both kept the foreign flavour of the original text and also offered new ways of speaking and thinking in the target work. So foreignization can both expect more from and present more to the reader. Foreignization, Grammenidis and Floros show, is a way for Greek translators, and thereby Greek readers, to show their difference from other, more powerful nations, and to allow 'meetings' or 'discoveries' (2019, pp. 336–7).

Although some of these examples suggest that foreignization often is the favoured method for covering the distance between source text and target reader, it is not the only way. A middle way is possible and may be preferred. For instance, Azadibougar and Haddadian-Moghaddam write, 'Much of the translation practice and discourse of the twentieth century [in Iran] have ensued from tensions between concern for the Persian language and fidelity to the source.[...] As such, a middle way is where the Persian translation tradition may be at best positioned, explored, and ideally criticized' (2019, p. 154). Travelling between domestication and foreignization may suit certain traditions or contexts, and could allow translators to best allow that meeting between reader and text.

3.4 Visibility

In the field of translation studies, Venuti developed the concept of visibility in 1995. There are two main aspects to this. One is the idea that the translator's labour should be visible within the actual text, that is that translators might choose strategies as they translate that make it clear to the reader that they are reading a translation. Another is the actual recognition a translator gets, which may include their name in/on the book, appropriate pay, awards and so on.

Translators who make a text more obviously foreign or different may force a reader to see that the text was not originally written in the target language. It is marked in a way that the original is not. And the inverse is true: if translators adopt a domesticating, smoothing approach to their work, then the translationness of target texts and the translators themselves will be virtually invisible.

Andrew Wilson discusses how Venuti has influenced people to think that readers should be aware of the work and the original culture, while some practising translators, such as the late Anthea Bell, say translators create an illusion and should not be seen. Wilson claims, 'This is where translation theorists and translation practitioners really part company' (2009, p. xvii). But do we really part company fully?

In recent times, the idea of translators' visibility in and of themselves, not just in terms of their work within the text, has been discussed more, not just in theoretical work such as Venuti's, but in society as a whole. For some translators, fair pay might be enough recognition. But for others, visibility goes beyond this. Some translators have agitated for their names to be on the covers of the books they translate and for them to be explicitly referred to in book reviews, among other things. In the UK, there has been a Name the Translator campaign (e.g. Stewart 2021, Anderson 2021). The open letter calling for translators to appear on the covers of book they translate reads

> For too long, we've taken translators for granted. It is thanks to translators that we have access to world literatures past and present.
> It is thanks to translators that we are not merely isolated islands of readers and writers talking amongst ourselves, hearing only ourselves. Translators are the life-blood of both the literary world and the book trade which sustains it. They should be properly recognised, celebrated and rewarded for this. The first step towards doing this seems an obvious one. From now on we will be asking, in our contracts and communications, that our publishers ensure, whenever our work

is translated, that the name of the translator appears on the front cover. (Society of Authors, n.d.)

Besides being visible on the cover of books, translators may also want to share literary awards with their authors (e.g. Estopace 2018) or indeed to be in line for prizes of their own (e.g. Anderson 2018).

There need not be a directly dichotomous choice between visibility and invisibility. Translators might want proper pay and public recognition, but choose to produce 'fluent' texts, or they might feel they do not want their names on the covers of books, but still approach their work 'ethnodeviantly', or favour any combination of who or what is visible in regard to a translation. I will return to the concept of middle ground below.

3.5 A New Concept: ish

Although some of the theoretical texts cited here do approach the complexity of the ideas of fidelity, equivalence, distance and visibility, when people discuss translation, I would suggest that there is still a general belief that there is a binary system; for example, a translation is either faithful or not, and a translator is either visible or not. Many of the students I have taught, who are beginning translators, have this view and are at times rather intransigent about it. But most things in life are not that simple; many concepts are on a spectrum, and there are lots of positions a translator and a text can take along that spectrum.

With that in mind, I would like to propose that translation studies adopt an idea from the world of sex advice and sex studies. Dan Savage has launched a number of new words and ideas into society at large. Among them is the term 'monogamish' (2021, pp. 64–7). It refers to people who are generally monogamous, but not always. Granted, the present book is not a sex advice manual but rather a text on translation, but I think there is some overlap. So the obvious question is: what does monogamish have to do with translation? To my mind, many people tend to think too rigidly about fidelity when it comes to translation. You are either faithful to a text and an author or an audience, or not. But, as Savage shows in regard to romantic and sexual relationships, this is quite limiting. You can be faithful in a wide range of ways to a work – to its sound, to the meaning of the words, to the style, to the overall function or intention, to its historical or cultural context and so on – but you may also need something of an open relationship. As a person and as a translator, you need some freedom. You can choose to primarily be with your spouse – to be faithful to the employment of metaphors in your text, for instance – and to also play around with someone else, perhaps the connotations of the words.

We have to stop expecting translators to be able to perform absolute fidelity. We know it is impossible, because there are so many aspects of a text that a translator needs to handle and each language and culture is different, which means the text cannot be kept exactly the same. As previously implied, if we want a translation to be precisely the same as the original, then it cannot actually be translated; it needs to be kept in the source language, in the same format. In other words, the only purely faithful translation is not a translation at all. I suggest we adapt Savage's concept of monogamish, or somewhere along a range of fidelity.

Similarly, in regard to equivalence, translators may need to free themselves up – to be swingers, maybe, or to try new positions or styles or toys, if we want to continue using Savage's work as a guide – in order to attempt to make their translation work equivalently in broader, perhaps even surprising ways. It may be that in order for a translation to affect readers in the way that the author and/or translator hope for, a translator might have to make more drastic, even 'aggressive', changes than would usually be the case. Translators need to feel that they have the flexibility to do that, without being held to strict ideas of equivalence being a one-to-one link between a word in the source language and a word in the target language.

Likewise, for distance, instead of a text having to be brought completely to the reader, or the reader being expected to always work hard to access the text, some traits or aspects of a text could be treated with domestication, while others with foreignization. The idea of monogamish is harder to apply to visibility in a sense, as a translator and/or their work cannot really be partially visible and partially invisible. However, it is true that translators have different preferences about this. All being well, publishers and authors would recognise the work translators do and would pay accordingly and would ensure translators are as visible as they like.

3.6 From Theory to Practice

This section has focused on a few of the areas of betweenness within translation, namely faithfulness, equivalence, distance and visibility. As noted already, there are many other ways in which translation is betwixt. It is between tongues and cultures, for example, it is between free and literal approaches, and it is between art, science and craft.

In some senses, the main thrust of this section appears to be a facile one: there are a number of ideas within translation theory that are often treated as though they are dichotomous, when in fact they are actually on a spectrum and translators should not feel as though they have to pedantically, meticulously choose and remain monogamously married to one method throughout an entire text, or even an entire translation practice. Rather, we should recognise that we can move along the spectrum. To return to the idea of a tightrope, which suggests that instead of shifting from one side of the dichotomy to the other, we have to somehow balance between options, we could actually say that as translators, we can allow ourselves to bounce on the tightrope and to feel the freedom of the air. Perhaps we could even let ourselves jump or fall off it at times, knowing there is (probably) a safety net beneath us and that we might see some astonishing things and amaze the audience as we fly.

Barton refers to this space between in a positive manner when she writes: 'That the topsy-turvy place between languages and cultures, which has been a site of humility and triangulation and self-knowledge, of absurdity and inanity and the best sort of creative fertility, can also offer, paradoxically, a kind of safety' (2021, p. 345). This is what we want when we translate – creativity, but also a sense that what we are doing is, in some sense, safe. I am not sure what she means precisely by safety, but I imagine safety from the sort of ethnocentric violence Venuti refers to, safety from postcolonialism or prejudice or an abuse of power, safety from being taken advantage of as people who work in the relatively unacknowledged and unsung field of translation, safety to be able to play around with our texts to the best of our ability and more.

So with each text you work on, consider your various allegiances, aims and audiences. Who or what are you an ally to? What sort of deviant are you or do you want to be? As translators, we have to become comfortable with living and working between languages, cultures, people, approaches, theories and so on, and we need to find our own way forward, backward, upward, downward and in every other possible direction.

Chapter 4
IDENTITY

Literary theorists have been analysing the importance of identity in recent decades, both in regard to the characters in books and to the people who write those works. For example, what is the nationality, ethnicity, religion, ideology, sexuality, gender or ability of a character or an author and how does it impact the way they write or are written about and how does it affect our understanding of the person and/or the text (e.g. see Bennett and Royle 2009, pp. 179, 199, 216, 234)? In translation studies, more recently, questions that have been raised include the following: Which authors get translated and why? Which authors are left only in their own language or in a select few other tongues? Who gets to become a translator and through what means? Who is invited to translate a given work and why are they considered the right or most appropriate translator for that particular text? Are there ways of challenging the choice of texts to translate and people to translate them? How does translation complicate ideas of nationality or other forms of identity? As Wilson notes, citing Peter Newmark, the 'views and prejudices of the translator, which may be personal and subjective, or may be social and cultural, involving the translator's "group loyalty factor," which may reflect the national, political, ethnic, religious, social class, sex, etc. assumptions of the translator' (2009, p. 54).

In this section, I will focus on some aspects of identity on a larger scale. I am not fully inclusive here due in part to word count restraints and in part because of a lack of research. An example of a missing topic is how someone's sexuality might affect how and what they translate, and how translation in turn might impact on understandings of sexuality; but perhaps what is explored here can inspire ideas about additional aspects of identity and their intersection with translation.

4.1 Translation as a form of Building National, Cultural and/or Linguistic Identity

Rita Kothari and Krupa Shah state that '[t]ranslation in the twentieth century has acquired this new role – of fostering group pride and history and also of enacting linguistic and cultural identities' (2019, p. 140). Translation, then, is not only a way of transferring information and ideas from one language or culture or another – although obviously that is important enough on its own – but also a chance to introduce people to other stories and histories, and an opportunity for those in certain groups to gain a sense of their own background. Writing generally serves this purpose; as Rudine Sims Bishop wrote some time back, literature provides 'mirrors' (reflections of ourselves), 'windows' (views into other people's lives) and 'sliding doors' (which 'readers have only to walk through in imagination to become part of whatever world has been created or recreated by the author') (1990, n.p.). We could suggest that translation is particularly important in this regard because of the intercultural aspect.

We are all products of our time and place and so are the texts that we produce. Why we choose to translate specific works, which languages we translate them to and how we translate them are sometimes a simple matter, such as that there is information written in one tongue that is needed in another. But in other cases, we may choose to translate from a place of pride or from wishing to educate people or expand their horizons. As some translation scholars have noted, this may stem from national, cultural or linguistic identity. It has even been found that translation affects our view of ourselves. For example, Basalamah describes translation's impact on Arab nationality (or, rather, pan-nationality) and culture. He discusses

> two major periods of Arab history, namely what I would broadly name 'The rise of the Self' and the (post) colonial 'surrender of the Self'. While acknowledging the contribution of Arab culture to humanity through translation, it is necessary to nuance the portrait of a past that is usually seen as ahistorical and artificially surviving in the collective imagination as a shining period that has continuously been shedding its lights until today. That is why it will be paramount to contrast that first period with the following section (the (post)colonial) which brings to the fore a very different picture, not only of translation, but of Arab self-perception through the new notion of translation [...]
> (2019, p. 172)

The notion raised here is that which texts have been translated and to which languages have led to an understanding of the self or to a 'surrender' of the self. If your culture focuses on texts translated from other languages, for instance, then this might lead you to believe that your people do not think deeply or produce important contributions to the world. Also, the texts that are translated to your language might influence your thinking, potentially in negative ways, perhaps causing you to not believe in your culture, language, religion and so forth to the extent you did before, or making you and your people lose confidence in yourselves. Additionally, even if many books are published in your language, if they are not translated to other tongues, you might begin to get the impression that you are not respected in other parts of the world and that your culture is lesser than others. This is part of the postcolonial aspect referred to here; when the flow of ideas goes one way only, this suggests a certain amount of power and (dis)respect (there is more on postcolonialism and power in the next section). Basalamah points to changing notions of translation in the Arab world and throughout Arab history which have impacted upon Arabs' sense of self, and suggests that with more translation, there could be more 'dignity, growth, self-fulfilment' for Arab people (2019, p. 173).

A similar case can be made for Hebrew, although interestingly this was perhaps especially the case at a time when Arabic was more highly regarded as the language of knowledge, which reveals how hierarchies shift over time, sometimes influenced by translation. Ben-Ari and Levin write that

> As Jews in Christian Europe began to discover the knowledge available to Arabic speaking Jews from Muslim Spain, there rose a demand for translation into Hebrew, the shared language that was up until then reserved for almost exclusive use in the religious domain. Important compositions in philosophy, mathematics, astronomy and medicine, among others, were translated into Hebrew, which needed a wide-scale broadening to allow for the expression of whole fields of knowledge it had never been used for before. In the case of translating Jewish works originally written in Arabic, such as Maimonides', translators' rhetoric often spoke of returning compositions into the (holy) tongue befitting their subject matter. Translation of secular knowledge started creating the needed vocabulary with which Hebrew could be made into a language fit for philosophic and scientific expression, allowing for further development in these fields to be written in Hebrew in the original. Translation of literature and poetry from Arabic provided new models for secular writing in Hebrew. (2019, p. 198)

That is to say, Jews wanted access to knowledge at a time when it was mainly available in Arabic, Latin or other tongues. While Jews have generally been multilingual (with Hebrew reserved for religious texts until modern times, with the founding of Israel, and other languages used on a daily basis in a secular way), for Jews in the Middle Ages, having works translated to Hebrew both gave them contact with those ideas and also signalled that Hebrew was a valued language and that Jews were a people on a par with others. This idea recurred in more recent times when Israel was being transformed into a modern nation-state. Ben-Ari and Levin say, regarding this

> the first Prime Minister, David Ben-Gurion, [announced] his translation project, or rather vision. Calling for the 'Foundation of the Spiritual State', he turned, in 1952, to renowned men of letters, asking for lists of masterpieces in philosophical writings recommended for translation. He himself suggested starting with Plato and Spinoza, then Buddha's conversations, the Upanishads, Greek and (some, select) Roman classics, Chinese philosophical literature, etc. In 1958, the 10th anniversary of the young state, he assembled a committee that was to first determine which spiritual world classics should be translated, in order to broaden the horizons of the Israeli reader, then find translators to undertake the enormous job. (2019, p. 205)

Translation, then, can help build nations, states and cultures. It can force the creation of new words and spread ideas. On a political level, this is hugely important. It also affects the language people have available to them and the way they speak and write.

A similar concept, in terms of building a (national) self and thereby a culture, comes from research from Iran. Here, though, the emphasis is on the other direction. Instead of primarily wanting others to learn about their culture, as important as that is, there is a sense in Iran that translation matters precisely because of the influence from other cultures – which some might call colonial, whereas others welcome it. Azadibougar and Haddadian-Moghaddam note that translation

> is a major player in contemporary Iranian culture. For one thing, the modernization discourse (i.e. translating in order to import modern, that is European/Western, ideas into Persian) has dominated the field of cultural production for long and has been a considerable motivation for translation. In addition, the status and prestige of translation in Iran is not only due to its connection with the modernization discourse, but to the internationally peripheral position of the Persian language […] the number of documents translated into Persian is much higher than the average number of documents translated from Persian into central or semi-peripheral languages. (2019, p. 156)

So more is translated to Farsi than from it but some view this as important because of its potential impact on modernising the nation.

Along with the discussion of nations and cultures, it is also important to acknowledge specific languages. Most cultures or countries have multiple languages and the choice of which language to translate from and which to translate to also makes a statement that can be both personal and more largely political. Kothari and Shah write about the many languages of India and say that in the history of translation in India, 'the choice to translate from non-classical (regional, bhashas) languages became a mark of established translators who saw a dynamic India living in languages spoken at homes and in bazaars, rather than courts and offices' (2019, p. 140). They cite how Sanskrit may have been seen as the historically important and literary tongue of India, while for some translators, it is more democratic and contributes more to national and personal identity to translate to and from vernaculars (ibid.). Both kinds of translation are needed, but it makes a statement when a translator chooses one language over another.

To look to the positive, besides helping to build nations, expand intellectual prospects, give people pride in their language and culture, and create new words, translation can also introduce new ways of writing, and thereby new ways of thinking. Returning to areas that speak Farsi, Azadibougar and Haddadian-Moghaddam state that, 'Translation introduced brand new prose genres into Persian literary tradition. For instance, before Persian writers wrote novels, the genre was translated from European languages into Persian. This led to a gradual change which increased the literary significance of prose, at the expense of verse that had dominated the literary system for centuries' (2019, p. 156). While some might find it problematic and indeed a colonial issue that styles of writing (and thus also beliefs about writing and literature more broadly) have been imported from one country to another, one could argue that this is how the exchange of ideas has worked throughout history, ideally with the flow going both ways, but also that Persian writers presumably could and did adapt the novel and other non-Persian genres and then moved them into the Persian context. In other words, translation here contributes to culture-building by bringing in new approaches to art and making different genres available.

These examples offer a sense that translation can challenge, develop, strengthen and affect identity. This can be identity in a small way, such as someone's understanding of themselves, or on a much larger scale, including pride in one's language or culture or the ability for people to express themselves. A new metaphor can be added here, namely translation as a form of construction, and translators therefore as builders of various kinds. Translators can help repair or construct from scratch languages, peoples, cultures and more.

4.2 From Theory to Practice

There are many possible intentions behind the translation of a given text or author and the choice of languages to be translated from and to. Aims and skopos (or functions, see Nord 1997, pp. 27–31) are as diverse as the translators, editors, publishers and others involved in the process of translation. But it has been clearly shown in this section that sometimes a translation takes place because of a desire to educate others about an identity or to expand an identity, or both, and the converse can be true too, with certain translations carried out in order to control or change an identity, personal, cultural, national or linguistic.

Where does this leave a translator? Besides thinking about how your translation may develop or constrict a culture, literature or language, also think about your own identity. Although here I have focused on identity in a larger sense, translation can also transform the identity of the text or writer or even translator. Writing about the poet and translator Seamus Heaney, Eugene O'Brien states that translation 'always differs/defers the movement of thought from point of origin to point of arrival' and that '[i]t is this process of transformation and transference that is ethically creative in Heaney's work, as it "complicates" notions of identity' (O'Brien 2001–2002, p. 24). A translator may find their identity shaken, challenged or transformed through the act of translation. O'Brien notes translation 'may lead to the possibility of some form of interaction between selfhood and alterity which allows one to get through the thicket of essentialist identity' (2001–2002, p. 34).

Translation both impacts identity and is impacted by identity. What effects do you want your work to have?

Chapter 5

POWER

To translate is to both have power and also to be under the command of others, and thus to be powerless. As translators, we have some say over which texts and authors we translate, and we can make decisions about how we translate particular words, concepts and characters and the texts in general, even if the authors or our editors or publishers sometimes make final decisions that we do not always agree with. We can sometimes choose whether to put our names on the end products or to distance ourselves from them and also whether to participate in the marketing of said texts. Our translations can have power over others and can make a difference, positive or negative. In short, translation is imbued with power, which flows in a variety of directions, and as translators, we must be aware of how we use (or abuse) that power and how we ourselves might be taken advantage of by others with (more) power.

In literary theory, the discussion of power stems in part from work on postcolonialism and feminism, and the consideration of these topics in relation to translation is more contemporary. In this section, I explore what translation theory has to say about power dynamics, briefly exploring postcolonial, feminist, queer and child-centred approaches, and how we can become more aware of power as we translate and work in the field of translation. It is important to recognise that this is not an exhaustive analysis of power in literature, language and society; there are fruitful ideas from many other fields, such as disability studies, fat studies or linguistics, that are worth exploring, though I do not have the space to do so here.

In many ways, translation is about othering and un-othering. Translation, in the best of all possible worlds, expands our horizons and brings us closer to one another. So how that happens and how we treat the other is of utmost importance. Hatim and Munday sum up some of the issues of power as follows

> In the context of translating or assessing translations, one sense of **power** involves using language to 'include' or 'exclude' a particular kind of reader, a certain system of values, a set of beliefs or an entire culture. One cannot help but notice how, in some sense, the bulk of foreign

literature translated into English and published in the west tends to sound the same, almost as though written by one writer and translated by one translator. This may indeed be explained in terms of translation 'universally' imposing its own constraints on the kind of language we use in translation (as opposed to original writing, for example). In **power** terms, however, this can also mean that somewhere, somehow, there is some exclusion of a reader (coerced to read in a particular way), an author (committed to oblivion) or a translator (doomed to be invisible). (2004, p. 93, emphasis original)

Who or what is included or excluded and how and what impact does this have? Is there anything we as translators can or should do about it?

5.1 Postcolonialism and Power

Postcolonialism explores, among other subjects, the relationships between the colonised nations and peoples and those who colonised them, and the aftermath of such colonisation. One aspect of colonisers wresting and retaining control was through language and literature, such as limiting which tongues could be employed in certain contexts or ensuring that particular books with the desired points of view were made available while less desirable ones were not. Colonisers may have genuinely believed in some circumstances that they were doing the colonised a service (such as 'educating' those who needed it, or offering what the colonisers believed was the true religion, for example Ashcroft 2001, p. 80 or Robinson 1997, p. 22), while in others, they were likely aware that they were taking advantage of a people who they deemed inferior in order to use their land, products, bodies and so on. Either way, controlling the flow of information was a clear way of promoting propaganda or preventing rebellion. Nicholas Dirks writes that 'in certain important ways, culture was what colonialism was all about' (1992, p. 3) and '[i]f colonialism can be seen as a cultural formation, so also culture is a colonial formation' (ibid.).

Susan Bassnett and Harish Trivedi state that 'the role played by translation in facilitating colonization is also now in evidence' (1999, p. 5). Robert Young writes

> Colonies began as translations, transpositions from the mother country to the unwritten *terra nulla*. Under postcolonial eyes, translation itself is transformed from a neutral space in which it parades as a practice of intercultural communication between individuals, 'only connect,' into an act of power and potentially a practice of domination between subjects

and the subjected. Translation becomes a form of appropriation, towards the end of political control, a practice of violence and domination.[...]

The colonial experience is thus defined through the procedures of being translated, hybridised, with the indigenous culture the target culture, and contrasted with the more active role of the postcolonial cultural translator. (2006, p. 28, italics original)

I do not believe translation is ever neutral. Román Álvarez and África Vidal helpfully note that

[t]ranslators are constrained in many ways: by their own ideology; by their feelings of superiority or inferiority towards the language in which they are writing the text being translated; by the prevailing poetical rules at that time; by the very language in which the texts they are translating are written; by what the dominant institutions and ideology expect of them; by the public for whom the translation is intended. (1996, p. 6)

I agree with Young that colonialism reminds us how language and translation can be employed for 'violence and domination', so one group can dominate another. As I wrote in earlier work, 'Cultures are translated from one place to another, just as texts are. Translation can be a metaphor for colonization, which means that translation within colonization is, in a sense, a double translation' (Epstein 2012, p. 14). Álvarez and Vidal too say that translation can 'be seen as reflecting the colonial experience; the source/original holds the power, the colony/copy is disempowered but placated through the myth of transparency and objectivity of the translation. The colony, in short, is perceived as a translation, never as an original, but this is concealed by a promise of equitable textual relations' (1996, p. 21).

Basalamah refers to a specific case when he explains how translation was (ab)used by the French in order to carry out a 'civilizing mission' on the Egyptians (2019, p. 181). They wanted 'French science and culture [to] be available to Egyptians in Arabic.[...] Egypt consecrates France because France seems to consecrate Egypt by its ability to speak' (ibid.). Basalamah sums up the negative power of translation by stating that 'the postcolonial perspective emphasizes the ruggedness of the consecration process as "violent". Here, the notion of translation betrays its inability to keep the parties engaged in the transaction as equals and demonstrates its inherent oppressive nature by pointing out not only its appropriating powers but also its self-alienating ones' (2019, p. 182).

However, if translation might be used for purposes – nefarious or otherwise – that we as translators might not recognise or support, we can do something about that. We can choose what to translate and how to translate, which can disrupt, subvert or challenge power relations (e.g. Hatim and Munday 2004, p. 109). Postcolonial approaches remind us that people who are in power, or who want to have power, can use a variety of methods to access and keep that power, and a non-physically violent (though intellectually and culturally violent) method is employing culture, including literature and language, to serve their aims; above, Venuti called this ethnoviolence. Postcolonial approaches help us 'understand the many ways power and authority are channelled, so that we can recognize them in our own societies and, when we find them unjust or tyrannical, fight back' (Robinson 1997, p. 88).

5.2 Child-Oriented Power

Many years ago, when I was reading about postcolonialism, it struck me that infantilising language was used to describe oppressed cultures and how people seemed to link the colonised with children. It seemed there was a sense that a group of people (such as adults or white, Christian Westerners) who knew better than another group (such as children or non-white, non-Christian people in the Global South) and that they believed they needed to teach and civilise and control them. The 'natives' or 'primitive people' are to be developed by the advanced people, the way children are developed by their parents and teachers; books, of course, are regularly employed to educate children and others. I explored the relationship between postcolonialism and children in depth in an earlier book (Epstein 2012), but I am not the only person to have noticed these linked ideas (cf. O'Sullivan 2005, p. 75, Oittinen 2000, Goldberg and Quayson 2002, p. xv or Nikolajeva 2010).

There is, to my mind, an intriguing connection between children and translation. Source texts come before target texts, and as we have seen some argue that the target text should be an 'equivalent' or 'copy' of the source. Likewise, some adults appear to feel that children are created as copies of their parents. Both the target text and a child come after the original, and perhaps are seen as therefore lesser than their forebears. The issues of control and power are thus pertinent to both translation and children.

There is an evident power imbalance when it comes to children. They may be perceived as having rights, such as those set out by the United Nations' Convention on the Rights of the Child, but those rights are not always and everywhere respected. Furthermore, it is always adults bestowing those rights. Children, as young activists, can and do speak up and challenge societal norms, but they are still reliant on adults, for example, to provide them with material to use for their protests or to take them to places where they can protest or give speeches, and adults certainly are the ones who need to institute change in society, at least in regard to changing laws or societal structures. In terms of texts, it is nearly always grown-ups who are responsible for writing, editing, translating, agenting, publishing, marketing, selling, buying, teaching and otherwise controlling access to the material. This means that what adults think about children as readers and as read-to and as members of a given society will impact how adults produce and make available literature for younger people.

Riitta Oittinen, whose work on translating for children has been very influential, writes that the 'primary task of the translator for children [is] to think of her/his future readers – children and adults reading aloud to their children' (2000, p. 28) and argues that translators should take into consideration the children's 'experiences, abilities, and expectations' (2000, p. 34). Zohar Shavit agrees writing that translators can carry out 'an adjustment of the text to make it appropriate and useful to the child, in accordance with what society regards (at a certain point in time) as educationally "good for the child"; and an adjustment of plot, characterization, and language to prevailing society's perceptions of the child's ability to read and comprehend' (2006, p. 26). While this belief could certainly be debated (e.g. Woodstein 2023, pp. 43–50), I would suggest that not all translators recognise the level of potential control and impact they have over their readers, both children and older ones.

Adults can and do abuse their power over children, whether by ignoring or eroding rights, or by writing or translating texts in a way that adds to their control or shapes readers or pushes them in a certain direction. It is also true that adults can and do abuse their power over other adults. Texts – both the original and the translation – and the various processes of production, including translation, are affected by the perspectives that writers and translators have of the readership. Age-based and child-centred theories can bring this into relief and remind us not to underestimate our readers or to feel that we always know better than they do.

5.3 Feminist Power

As second-wave feminism developed, feminist and gender-aware ideas began to permeate literary studies. Scholars began to explore who produced and published what sort of work and how the various genders were depicted within those texts. As Andrew Bennett and Nicholas Royle discuss, gender stereotypes may permeate how people write (and, I would add, translate). They give an example of 'binary oppositions', where the female character is depicted in literature as passive, lacking in control, perhaps hysterical, while the male is active, dominant and rational (1960/2014, p. 179). Bennett and Royle state that '[a]ll literary texts can be thought about in terms of how they represent gender difference and how far they may be said to reinforce or question gender-role stereotypes' (1960/2014, p. 180), but they also point out that this can be reductive and that more subtle readings are needed too (1960/2014, p. 182).

Indeed, we must go beyond the readings of texts to explore the writing, production and translation of them as well, although indubitably reading and interpreting is the first step in translation. Feminist translation studies have done just that, looking for ways of challenging and subverting gender in texts as translators translate them. Feminist translation scholars, such as Luise von Flotow (1991, 1997, 2011) and Sherry Simon (1996), have developed a variety of what they term feminist translation strategies. Carol Maier states that a feminist strategy is shaped by a 'simultaneous affirmation and refusal', which means 'affirming women writers through a refusal to translate work written by men, often choosing to translate only explicitly feminist texts' (1998, p. 99). Perhaps regardless of the gender of the author or the feminist standpoint – or lack thereof – of the text, there are strategies that translators can employ while working. These include supplementing, prefacing and footnoting, and hijacking (Simon 1996, p. 14), while translator Suzanne de Lotbiniére-Harwood uses notes or radical changes, such as invented spellings (Conacher 2006, p. 250). Kim Wallmach lists 'substitution, repetition, deletion, addition and permutation' (2006, p. 15), and further sub-methods, such as 'compensation by footnoting' and 'compensation by splitting' (2006, p. 18), and Castro and Ergun also refer to translators adding in female characters (2018, p. 129), or choosing to using gender-inclusive language, such as when translating religious texts (2018, p. 130).

Von Flotow notes, 'Translation makes deliberate choices about which writer to translate, which foreign ideas and materials to disseminate. These choices are premeditated, planned and carefully evaluated, and the meticulous word-by-word labour of translation is often equally self-aware. In other words, translation, it can be argued, is as intentional, as activist, as deliberate as any feminist or otherwise socially-activist activity' (2011, p. 4). The concept of deliberation is particularly key here, in that it suggests that translators must be conscious and conscientious when working, analysing texts and making choices in an intentional manner. Feminist translators continue to try to ensure that a variety of texts are chosen to be translated, rather than solely works by men and/or works that present stereotyped views of the genders, and the strategies they developed are widely applicable and stimulating to consider.

5.4 Queer Power

As with feminist writing and translating, all forms of power-aware work translators might undertake could draw attention to certain subjects (such as by highlighting or even adding them in), or they can remove them (as through deletion or changing them), and/or problematising and discussing them (as in footnotes or introductions). Queer approaches to translation likewise focus on a potentially problematic area of a text and make conscious choices about how to handle them. I think of this as translators choosing queer or queery translation.

Terminology is tricky here, so before delving more into what I call queer translation strategies, I must pause briefly to acknowledge that some people dislike or are offended by the term 'queer'. I do not have the space to discuss this in depth, but my personal view – as both a queer person myself and as someone who has worked and taught in the field for a long time – is that queer is a useful umbrella term. I also like that by using it, we are taking it back from those who wish to employ it as an insult. I do often use it interchangeably with LGBTQ+, with the plus sign signalling inclusion and openness (see Epstein and Chapman 2021, p. 2 or Woodstein 2023, pp. 28–31 for more on terminology).

In previous research, I wrote, 'LGBTQ writers and translators may look at the ways in which the heteronormative society in which we live influences how we write and translate, and are beginning to think about how to fight against and subvert this heterosexism' (Epstein 2017, pp. 120–1). I went on to propose

> Queer translators/translators of queer texts can […] focus on the queerness of a character or a situation, or they can push a reader to note how a queer character is treated by another character or by the author, or they can otherwise 'hijack' a reader's attention by bringing issues of sexuality and gender identity to the fore. Such strategies can be called 'acqueering', as they emphasise or even acquire queerness. For example, a translator can add in queer sexualities, sexual practices, or gender identities or change straight/cis identities or situations to queer ones; remove homophobic, biphobic, or transphobic language or situations or highlight it in order to force a reader to question it; change spellings or grammar or word choices to bring attention to queerness; or add in footnotes, endnotes, a translator's preface, or other paratextual material to discuss queerness and/or translatorial choices.
>
> On the other hand, a translator may choose – or be encouraged by the publisher to choose – strategies that remove or downplay queer sexualities, sexual practices, gender identities, or change queerness to the straight/cis norm. Doing so can be considered 'eradicalisation', as this eradicates the radical nature of queerness. (2017, p. 121)

The two – admittedly slightly ridiculously named – terms, acqueering and eradicalisation, could be seen as queer-focused versions of foreignization and domestication, or of Venuti's ethnodeviance and ethnoviolence. In other words, they can force readers to come to the text and to be confronted by queerness, or they can violently move the text to a certain swathe of the readership by smoothing out the queer elements. This is a spectrum of strategies, however, not a dichotomy. Emphasising, removing or otherwise changing aspects of a work due to the queerness, or lack of queerness, in it relates to the translator's own ideology as well as the publisher's view of what is best for their audience and their bottom line, and so is saturated with people's opinions about LGBTQ+ topics, and they can use their power to inflict their views on others.

Shalmalee Palekar calls the translation of queer literature either 'interventionist' or 'repressive' (2017, p. 12), which are similar in meaning to my own terms but which perhaps more than my own highlight the power a translator has. William M. Burton prefers the term 'inversion' and defines it as 'a turning of the text against itself: inverting the hidden power relations of heterosexism by revealing and underscoring them through techniques borrowed from feminists' (2010, p. 57). The power that was previously 'hidden' is thereby brought into the light through such translations.

5.5 From Theory to Practice

The theories referred to above look at power from a variety of perspectives – race, culture and ethnicity, age, gender and sexuality, as well as in terms of language, censorship and norms – but as already noted, there are other approaches and other ways of understanding power. What is important is to generally have a perspective on the role power can play in writing and translating literature, and then specifically to be able to think about it as we translate each individual author and work. As Bassnett and Trivedi point out, 'translation is a highly manipulative activity that involves all kinds of stages in that process of transfer across linguistic and cultural boundaries. Translation is not an innocent, transparent activity but is highly charged with significance at every stage; it rarely, if ever, involves a relationship of equality between texts, authors or systems' (1999, p. 2).

Translations are important as a way of breaking down barriers and providing information. As translators, we could be justified in being proud of the work we are carrying out. But we also have to remember that we do hold some power. We could ask: Why have I in particular been chosen to translate this work? What power do I personally have in regard to this translation task? As we accept translation assignments and translate the texts, we should consider issues such as whether the text actually needs to be translated, why it is being translated from a specific language/culture to another, whether translation is one way between those two languages/cultures or whether it is bidirectional and whether the text is going to be used as a form of propaganda or control. We can also take inspiration from postcolonial, feminist, queer and other ideas about power in order to recognise the way power is channelled in texts, including translated ones. We might analyse who has gotten published and selected for translation, whether stereotypes are employed in a work, whether certain voices, ideas or people are focused on or ignored, which audience/s a text is aimed at and how this might change in translation, and other such points.

Von Flotow says that 'socially-activist and implicitly feminist approaches that examine identity, power and visibility continue to bear fruit' (2011, p. 9), but I think we could substitute any power-aware approach for 'feminist'. To put it simply, translators need to keep in mind what we are translating, for whom (both client and end user) and why, and what our role is in this so that we can best decide how to use our power and which strategies to employ while translating.

Chapter 6

ETHICS

This section in many ways brings together many of the theoretical ideas that came before. What translation is, what translators do, how the identity of the author and translator influences the decisions made and so on all relate to the idea of ethics. In the simplest sense, ethics are the values or morals that shape someone's behaviour. While the term today often refers to the 'philosophical study of the concepts of moral right and wrong and moral good and bad, to any philosophical theory of what is morally right and wrong or morally good and bad, and to any system or code of moral rules, principles, or values' (Singer 2022, n.p.), it is also the case that '[e]*thics* and *morality* are now used almost interchangeably in many contexts' (Singer 2022, n.p., italics original).

In a translatorial context, someone's ethics might influence what jobs they choose to take on, how they translate the work in question, how they relate to the author, client or audience, whether they put their name to their translation, whether and how they promote the work and so on. We do not translate in a vacuum, however, so it is not always just a choice of whether to take on that assignment or not; sometimes we are affected by, for instance, our need to earn money to support our family, or the fact that a particular translation was assigned to us by a teacher or employer and not something we agreed to independently or would have chosen for ourselves. Also, of course, many translators are members of translators' associations, which often have their own codes of conduct and guidelines, and these rules or suggestions may clash with translators' own preferences or values.

Schwimmer suggests that the 'third language' of translation 'is fundamentally ethical' (2017, p. 57), with the first two languages presumably the source and target tongues. And yet, despite how important ethics are to translation, the subject has not been extensively studied or written about

> While the descriptive approach did transform Translation Studies into a properly scientific discipline with its new conceptual framework and methodology, it ended up neglecting an essential dimension of the experience of various participants in the translation process, that of

> the sometimes excruciating feeling that a given translation solution, or a given choice of how to – in a more general sense – behave during the translation process, might somehow be right or wrong, better or worse than other solutions, other choices. Descriptivism was simply not very helpful in triggering reflections or offering solutions to how to deal with those ethical issues that invariably arise during the working day of a translator or interpreter (or editor, proofreader, etc.). (Greenall, Alvstad, Jansen and Taivalkoski-Shilov 2019, p. 640)

In other words, even though scholars have been working to describe what translators do as they are translating and the impact of this on the text, they have not always reflected on why translators have felt compelled to make certain choices, leading to ethics being a 'neglected' subject. Still, it is a growing area of analysis. Alberto Fuertes states that the 'first contributions on professional ethics include essays and articles published throughout the 1990s and into the early twenty-first century' (2019, p. 420) He further notes, 'Ethics has been a key concept in the development of Feminist Translation Studies first and, more recently, of Queer Studies' (2019, p. 424, capitals original), which suggests that perhaps it is viewed as being more relevant to certain texts or subjects. He adds that in the Spanish context, in particular, scholars are exploring the ethics and politics of translating sex and sexuality, among other subjects. But even if theorists have begun working on this subject, there is still much more to do. As translators, we must reflect on our own values, those of the society we live in and those of any associations we belong to or belief systems we subscribe to.

Therefore, in this section, I explore what translation theory has to say about translatorial ethics, the role of both personal and professional ethics, how ethics might affect the everyday work of translators as well as some examples of ethics in action. As you will notice, there are clear links to discussions in other chapters, which shows how related most of these topics are. For example, ethical values often are connected to our identity; personal mores likely impact our professional behaviour. So it can be hard to tease out what is influencing a translator at any given time. Nonetheless, here the focus will be on a translator's personal beliefs and on the professional guidelines they may have to follow as a member of a given association, among other ethical topics.

6.1 Personal Ethics

It is important to acknowledge that we are all products of our environment. While we can and do deeply reflect upon the values we have been taught by our parents, teachers, religions, political leaders and so on, and we can choose whether to accept or reject them, we are also confined by the historical period and cultural and legal contexts in which we live. So although this section refers to personal ethics, perhaps it is more accurate to use the term societally influenced personal ethics. If we translate according to personal ethics that are not generally approved of or that are disagreed with by our client, the translation may be changed or not published, or we might not get paid. And worse, if we make a choice that goes against a legal or religious framework, we may face mortal consequences, such as William Tyndale did; he was executed for even daring to translate the bible (Britannica 2023, n.p.). Part of what is interesting when it comes to all this is that personal ethics have not been recognised until recently as part of translation.

Pym argues that 'Mutual trust, understanding, and commitment cannot be preconditions for translation – they should be the long-term aims' (Pym 2012, p. 60). This suggests that a translator and their client should have a relationship where they both are committed in some way to one another and to the text and can understand and trust each other. This certainly seems ideal and should be a 'long-term aim', but it is obviously not always realistic. Pym discusses the translator's 'responsibility to the matter' (2012, pp. 76–7), 'responsibility to the client' (2012, pp. 77–8) and 'responsibility to the profession' (Pym 2012, pp. 79–81). This implies that the translator's decisions need to be led by their sense of duty to the work, the client and to translation as a whole. I would add that the translator also needs to consider the reader (who could be perceived as the end client ultimately) and society generally, beyond translation as a profession. Pym emphasises that the 'translation form posits that the translator is responsible for some things but not for others' (Pym 2012, p. 67). If translators have all these responsibilities, we must understand the 'principles', or values, that shape what they do.

Phillippa May Bennett writes that when translators and scholars have broached the subject of ethics, the concepts have included faithfulness, loyalty, accountability, responsibility and so on (2021, p. 31). Early on, 'translating ethically was equated with linguistic *equivalence*' (2021, p. 34, italics original) and this developed into the concept of being loyal and 'accountable to the author of the source text, the client or commissioner, the target audience and the profession' (ibid.), along the lines of what Pym suggests above (and cf. Fuertes 2019, p. 419). Citing Andrew Chesterman, Bennett notes that 'this type of ethics confers a certain invisibility upon the translator as they are merely fulfilling the clients' orders' (2021, p. 34). The translator's agency is thus ignored, as is their personality. They are doing what they are told, almost as if they are robots, acting automatically on instructions from others. Bennett points out that views began to change about this; ethics began to encompass foreignization and to be against fluency, unless they 'cause cultural divisions and a cultural elite, thus actually becoming unethical' (2021, p. 35). The next development was about 'social responsibility' (2021, p. 36) and contributing towards 'a more socially equal and fair world' (2021, p. 37). While the change from invisibility towards visibility, such as through foreignization, at least shows more awareness of the person behind the translation, it is clear that nonetheless, there is a strong belief that it is the translator who is responsible to others when it comes to translation.

There is something very obvious missing from these discussions: who has responsibility to or for the translator? Perhaps the starting point for an answer is the translator. In other words, the translator needs to take responsibility for the choices they make in their career and with specific texts. So many outward-looking duties are placed upon the translator, but they should have the right to search inwards as well. And while obviously there should be more discussion of the duty of others towards translators – for example, a duty to pay them on time and to give them the fee agreed upon, to name them on the translation and publicity materials, to treat them with respect, to allow them to see any changes before the work is published and so on – here I am focusing on the translator and their own ethics.

A translator's personal ethics can, as some of the examples later in this section show, cause them to make decisions about what to translate and how to translate it; for instance, a text might make them uncomfortable, so they reject the offer to translate it, or they might add, delete or change words to make the text more appropriate (appropriateness and propriety are slippery concepts) for their culture or readership or to fit better with their own beliefs. These are individual choices, but translation as a whole can be viewed as ethical from a personal perspective. For instance, O'Brien, writing about the poet and translator Seamus Heaney, discusses the ethical necessities involved in translating. Translation, for Heaney and for others who have the privilege to be choosy about publishers and texts (as Heaney does, but many translators do not, 2001–2002, p. 24), 'is metonymic of the ethical imperative: it is the quintessential form of dialogue with the other' (2001–2002, p. 25). Making the decision to translate is a way of engaging with a different person, culture or set of views; it is political and ideological. Haidee Kruger and Elizabeth Crots agree, saying that 'translational ethics is a matter of the agency of the translator in the wider socio-cultural and ideological sense. This agency, with its greater visibility, freedom and creativity, is not an end in itself – it brings with it greater ethical responsibility' (2014, p. 153). Again, this brings us back to the concept of responsibility; choice, power and privilege all come with responsibilities, as already noted. Seamus Heaney views this as not speaking out but rather speaking in (2001–2002, p. 25), bringing in other voices and ideas into his language. Perhaps it could be said that the ethical standpoint for Heaney, as well as for some other translators, is to reach across linguistic and cultural borders.

A translator's role in activism or social justice is a growing area of discussion within translatorial ethics. 'Activism and engagement in translation – this wider socio-cultural and -political role of translators – may therefore be regarded as part of professional ethics, as Cronin (2003) views it, or more properly as part of the translator's personal ethics, as Chesterman (2001) sees it' (Kruger and Crots 2014, p. 149; cf. Fuertes 2019, p. 422). Polly Barton questions the idea of activism when she asks whether translation is 'frivolous' or 'a form of activism' (2021, pp. 342–3) and says that 'as the world burns and crumbles, I wonder if sitting around adding to the pile of texts people feel obliged to read is where it is at – if this is comfortable inaction dressed up as virtue' (2021, p. 343). While her questioning is rational in the difficult times in which we live, I would still argue that translation's activist impulse is important. O'Brien refers to Heaney's 'ethical reaching towards discourses of otherness' (O'Brien 2001–02, p. 22), which is a useful way of summing up much of the discussion on the personal ethics of translating.

As Kruger and Crots discuss, there are different ways of delineating various aspects of translatorial ethics. They cite Chesterman's work extensively, and their review is useful

> Chesterman (2001) puts forward four models of translation ethics: an ethics of representation, an ethics of service, an ethics of communication, and norm-based ethics. As far as the ethics of representation is concerned, this is based on loyalty towards the source text, as well as loyalty towards ethical representation of the Other (Chesterman 2001:139–140). An ethics of service is founded on a view of translation as a service rendered to a client, and in this view ethical behaviour equates to meeting the ideals of rendering a professional service (Chesterman 2001:140). An ethics of communication is less concerned with representation of the source text, or meeting the client's requirements; rather it is founded on the principle of enabling communication and cooperation.[…] Lastly, Chesterman distinguishes a norm-based ethics, which is premised on the idea that norms encode the ethical values held at a particular time in a particular society, and that ethical behaviour therefore equates to behaving in accordance with these norms as socially sanctioned expectations. (Chesterman 2001, p. 141; 2014, p. 151)

Chesterman's views link in part to the activist impulses mentioned earlier, but also return to the idea of translators having a long list of duties – perhaps even loyalty, a word that Kruger and Crots employ (2014, p. 149, and cf. Nord 2007). Translators' work thus includes representing the text and author, serving the client (whoever that may be), 'enabling communication' between people, and translating according to ethical norms, perhaps in both the source and target cultures. Again, much of this seems idealistic and worth aiming for, but also at times ignores a translator's own responsibility to themselves and their own morals and beliefs.

Moira Inghilleri and Carol Maier refer to 'personal integrity' (1998/2011, p. 100), and the idea of integrity led me to expect to find more material about how professional ethics might lead a translator to carry out research or to treat the text in a particular way, but that was not something that came up often in the research. In her article about translating *Detransition, Baby* to Swedish, Julia Gillberg writes about how she could relate to the characters in Torrey Peters' novel, even though she herself is not trans. She hesitated before translating it as she did not share that lived experience but ultimately felt that 'translation is always about inviting in what is foreign to us' (2022, p. 13, my translation). Gillberg describes her process, which included quite a lot of research and some guesswork (2022, p. 14), and which ultimately involved collaboration with someone from the trans community in Sweden (2022, p. 15). This man looked over Gillberg's translation, corrected some word choices and gave more context to what it means to be trans in Sweden and how trans people themselves would use language (2022, pp. 16–7). In other words, for Gillberg, translating ethically involves research and contact with the community/culture in question.

In any piece of writing, it is more or less impossible to include ideas from all the scholars who have worked in that particular area. As I worked through my choices about whom to include and why, I mostly made the decisions based on what was most pertinent and what fit into the topics I discuss in this book. In one case, however, I made a choice based on my own personal ethics. I deliberately decided not to include work by a well-known scholar who has, in my opinion, made unacceptable political comments and has behaved in ways that have been perceived by myself and others as antisemitic. I did not feel that their name and work needed more publicity and I felt uncomfortable aligning myself with them in the way that I would have done if I had quoted from them (even if I had disagreed with and challenged their ideas). To me, this felt like it was the right decision to make, based on my values and beliefs, particularly around diversity, inclusivity and academic freedom, although a peer reviewer disagreed. Most scholars do not have the word count to discuss their choice of quotations and it is only in certain circumstances where it is absolutely essential to explore the topic in any depth – for instance, if a quite dated work is still relevant and useful although readers might wonder at its inclusion, or if there is a conflict of interest that must be disclosed – but I thought that as this section is on personal ethics, it was helpful to point out that they can guide decisions in scholarship, even if we do not usually discuss that.

There are many strong reasons to translate, not least as a way of engaging with and giving voice to and understanding and in turn being changed by the 'other', as in Heaney's work and perceptions, but it is also important to acknowledge that there is more to personal ethics than this.

6.2 Professional Ethics

While acknowledging the values a translator holds dear personally, it is also important to recognise that we cannot always hew to them. We are, for better or for worse, also affected by the place and time in which we live, the education we have received, instructions from the clients, the legislation and moral values of our country and culture and more. And beyond these general views on translation and these various influences on our work, if we choose to join one or more translators' associations, we may also be asked to agree to a specific code of conduct or set of guidelines that will shape our work as translators. We may work alone as translators, but we are part of a profession, and there may not be as much room for independent thought and decision-making if you are required to follow a set of ethics or rules you did not choose. Kruger and Crots define professional ethics as 'circumscribing an ethics informed by the immediate professional context in which the translation is commissioned and produced. Professional ethics is codified in codes of ethics or conduct, and constitutes an articulation of ethical obligations that is determined by an external locus of control – the profession and its associated norms and expectations.[…] Professional ethics is thus expressed from a professional subject position' (2014, p. 154).

As Kruger and Crots state, 'in the everyday setting of most translators' work, the concept of 'ethics' is usually invoked within the formal discursive framework of a code of practice, conduct or ethics' (Kruger and Crots 2014, p. 148), although, I am not convinced that such codes are always the most influential in terms of translatorial decision-making.

Fuertes writes that '[r]esearch on deontology (professional ethics) abounds, especially from the 2000s, and is mostly with reference to legal and institutional translation settings, with some innovative work on the role of interpreters in healthcare, in prisons and in court. Little new research has been done on literary ethics' (2019, p. 417). In other words, there is an awareness that it is an important subject, but it has not been analysed much within literary translation, a surprising gap.

Bennett discusses professional ethics as a group of rules decided upon by an organisation, which translators have to agree to abide by in order to be in the association (what happens if someone does not follow the rules is not always clear, nor is it always known if there is a repercussion for someone who breaks the code of conduct). For translators' associations, Bennett writes, ethics has a 'mainly practical and non-theoretical focus' and their codes of conduct 'have focused overwhelmingly on principles such as honesty, integrity, linguistic competence, confidentiality and trust' (2021, p. 32).

Bennett goes on to analyse several translators' associations' codes, which include guidelines about not fixing 'objectional language' or not having 'personal, private, religious, political or financial interests [that] conflict with their duties and obligations to their clients' (2021, p. 39), using re-creation as a strategy only if permitted by the client (2021, p. 41) and so forth. The key ethical concerns – or, at least, they can be considered key because they were mentioned in each of the codes Bennett explores – appear to be 'faithful', 'equivalence', and 'confidentiality' (2021, p. 43). Bennett actually suggests that fidelity and equivalence do not belong in codes of conduct (2021, p. 46); I too do not consider them strictly ethical.

In the previous section, activism came up frequently, as if it is perhaps a primary ethical concern for translators. Kruger and Crots note that despite the sense that these social duties are vital for the world of a translator, 'This broader view of the translator's ethical rights and responsibilities, however, is not generally emphasised in professional codes of conduct. Many practitioners (as well as scholars) believe [...] that political activism and engagement do not form part of professional ethics' (Kruger and Crots 2014, pp. 148–9). That suggests that the sociocultural role played by translators and all that this involves is placed squarely on the translators themselves, rather than being perceived as a matter of professional ethics. This implies a clear division, but of course things are not that clear-cut, and some would challenge the idea that the professional and the personal are separate. Fuertes writes that '[r]esearch on social ethics and translation has seen some attempts to initiate debate on the issue [and] in the context of globalization to question translators' authority, the idea of what 'responsible' translation is, and the ethical limits of the role of translators' (2019, p. 423). Fuertes describes an apparent attempt to formalise the ethical role of activism in translators' work (ibid.), but this has not had a broader reach, as far as I can tell from the scholarship.

Besides the translators' codes, as discussed here, there are also constrictions and guidelines created by a translator's contract with their client. If they have a contract, they will be duty-bound, ethically and legally, to follow it, or they may face consequences. It is also worth pointing out that in some countries or languages, there may not be translators' associations, and there could also be other elements within the culture that affect how translators work. So professional ethics is a bigger question than codes of conduct. For example, Azadibougar and Haddadian-Moghaddam call Iran 'ethically subversive' for the way it treats translation. They write

> Iran is member of the World Intellectual Property Organization (WIPO), but her absence in the UCC or similar conventions has gradually given a special shape to the Persian translation tradition – making it ethically subversive. This subversion has manifested itself in at least three ways. First, it has given maximum liberty to translators and publishers to select and publish books with no legal obligations to the authors or publishers of original works; as such, copyright has almost never been an initial concern or norm for translation or publication. Second, it has contributed significantly to retranslations, though in the absence of reliable empirical studies, it is hard to determine whether retranslations have been motivated more by quality issues or commercial incentives. Third, and this is yet to be acknowledged, it has prevented Iran from playing a more active role in the circulation of books and its literatures (if not ideas) on the global stage, either through translation of Persian books into other languages, or by active participation in the international book fairs where rights are negotiated. (2019, p. 158)

While much of their analysis is about the ethics of copyright and the legality of how publishers and translators work, the professional-cultural view of translation in Iran means that translators have a certain liberty involved in their work. However, they are also strongly influenced by censorship in their society. Azadibougar and Haddadian-Moghaddam show that for translators in Iran, their translatorial choices will be controlled to a certain extent by the ethics and norms of their society (2019, p. 160). This is true for many translators around the world.

Although I agree that we need an in-depth discussion about translators' codes of conduct, who they serve, what purpose they serve and what should be included in them, I also know that not all translators are members of translators' associations, nor do they all necessarily want to follow codes set by other people. In addition, as the example of Iran shows, professional ethics is a category that encompasses much more than codes of conduct; translators may be constricted or liberated – both of which appear to be the case in Iran, given the copyright rules or lack thereof and the religious precedents – by other aspects of society. So what I will return to now is how people view their own ethics and their feelings about what they do.

6.3 The Impact of Translatorial Ethics

Whether translators are bound by codes of conduct, influenced or constricted or liberated by their culture, or predisposed to certain ideas or beliefs because of their own experiences and backgrounds, or some combinations thereof, there will be an impact from their personal and professional ethics on their work. Some scholarship has explored translatorial choices in the light of ethics, with interesting results.

Annjo K. Greenall, Cecilia Alvstad, Hanne Jansen and Kristiina Taivalkoski-Shilov, referencing Chesterman, note that key points seem to be 'how to represent authors' intentions/texts in the best way, how to handle the otherness of the source culture/author/text in a respectful manner, how to best take into account the interests of commissioners and other recipients of translated texts, and how to bring culturally-specific values and norms to bear on ethical thinking and behavior' (2019, p. 640). In a study of translatorial decision-making, Kruger and Crots looked at, among other things, a text aimed at children. The translators were asked to work on 'pages [that] dealt with children's questions about same-sex relationships' (2014, p. 157). They stated that '[s]ince adults generally have distinct ideas about what is appropriate for children, it was expected that an emotional rather than a professional response would be elicited. It was predicted that some respondents might be in favour of educating children about this topic and would thus choose to translate literally, while other translators might find the topic inappropriate for the target audience and thus refuse to translate' (ibid.). Some of their interview subjects refused to translate this text (2019, p. 166); indeed, 30% said this was because it was, to their minds, 'inappropriate for or offensive to a particular target audience' (2019, p. 167), which links to the discussion of age and power earlier in this book. Kroger and Crots state, 'it appears that formal, informational texts are less likely to prompt a refusal to translate, and children's literature containing potentially inappropriate material is most likely to provoke this response' (Kruger and Crots 2014, p. 177). Meanwhile, some translators chose not to translate a text for adults because it offended their 'feminist beliefs' (2014, p. 160–1). Regardless of the audience, for many, the refusal to translate stemmed from their own personal ethics (2019, p. 169), and seemed in conflict with the professional ethics referred to above and as discussed by Greenall, Alvstad, Jansen and Taivalkoski-Shilov: 'when the strategy of refusal to translate was chosen it was overwhelmingly the consequence of personal ethics, with personal ethics cited 93% of the time

(40 out of 43 times) for this translation strategy, and professional ethics accounting for only 7% of motivations (3 out of 43 times)' (Kruger and Crots 2014, p. 166).

It is worth pointing out that Kroger and Crots did have a variety of findings, in part because they used a number of examples, some of which featured sexism or racism. Some translators felt they had to translate what was on the page, regardless of content – this could be seen as professional ethics and their sense of responsibility towards the requirements of their job – while others believed that they had to make changes because something was unacceptable for the readership. Intriguingly, experienced translators were more likely to stick with the text as written (75% of the time, in Kroger and Crots' study), while less experienced translators were around twice as likely as more experienced ones to choose strategies such as 'neutralising adaptation and refusal to translate' (2014, p. 173). It is not exactly clear why there was such a big difference, but '[i]t may be that the more experienced translators have been conditioned to behave in a certain way by professional exposure, whereas less experienced translators are still developing a style and might be less aware of what the conventional views of professional conduct are or what is expected of them in accordance with codes of conduct' (Kruger and Crots 2014, p. 173). Another reason could be that more experienced, presumably older, people have seen more of life and are less easily offended, protective or cautious; much more research would be needed to see if this is true of translators, because one could imagine this going either way, with some older people more set in their ways and others more relaxed.

Some of the examples here – such as refusing to translate non-heterosexuality – imply that there are personal ethics that lead translators to make what could be considered activist decisions. Pym might suggest that those translators are in the wrong, as he argues that 'the translator should tend to favor the weaker participants' (Pym 2012, p. 152). Pym offers himself as an example, stating that when translating for the President of Catalonia, he always chooses to emphasise Catalan and Catalonia and to favour that side of the exchange (i.e. over Spain as a whole, making decisions about Catalonia) (2012, pp. 152–3). One could say that anyone who is not in the majority, such as LGBTQ+ people, or people from certain religions or backgrounds, is 'weaker' and should be prioritised, given Pym's opinion about how certain activist ethics should guide translators. But as Kroger and Crots' study shows, this is not what actually happens, because obviously people vary in who they think is 'weaker' and what they consider appropriate. As Greenall, Alvstad, Jansen and Taivalkoski-Shilov state, 'sometimes voices *clash*, both externally and internally to translated texts, owing to conflicting interests, cultural differences and varying conceptions of what constitutes good and bad practice in translation and interpreting, as well as good and bad practice in the professional areas in which the translators and interpreters carry out their work' (2019, p. 641, italics original). While some translators make choices based on what they think is 'good and bad practice' and 'good and bad' for their readership, Kroger and Crots find that 'translation strategies premised on faithful translation are by far the preferred choice [...] when faced with ethically challenging material' (2014, p. 177), which might be read as implying that translators do not allow their personal ethics to override their professional ethics as much as ideas about activism and translation lead us to believe. Greenall, Alvstad, Jansen and Taivalkoski-Shilov sum this up by stating, 'most of the translators perceived that they have the freedom to follow their personal ethics, although this ethics went strongly in the direction of desiring to provide a faithful text, showing that in practice it may not be that easy to distinguish between telos (inner voices) and the external pressure of norms' (2019, p. 644). This obviously leads us once again to question fidelity.

Pym suggests that, 'For many prescriptive ethics of translation, you should do everything you can to avoid all possible errors. Unlimited effort seems to go hand-in-hand with ideal faithfulness. The translator should know everything, confirm everything, and explain everything. These prescriptions forget that the work is not free; it is exchanged for value of some kind' (Pym 2012, p. 133). Of course, translation studies have moved away from prescription towards description, but ethics could be seen as prescriptive in some circumstances. Translators do not generally work in situations where they can provide 'unlimited' effort and time, but in fact have to deal with a variety of pressures and beliefs, some of which will seem prescriptive. For example, codes of conduct are prescriptive, ideas about what is appropriate or not for a given audience or culture are prescriptive and personal views of acceptability are prescriptive. It is true that work is not free in regard to value, but it is also not free from prescriptions, even if some scholars within translation studies think we have left some of that behind. A number of examples mentioned above show that translators cannot easily dismiss the influence of either professional or personal ethics (and arguably there is not always an obvious distinction between personal and professional anyway [Kruger and Crots 2014, p. 150]).

Given that translators have their own ethics, biases and constraints, they must at least remember that 'the receiver *believes* the translation fully represents an anterior text. This belief – illusion, or indeed lie – is often false or ideologically quite easily manipulated. Yet that is what the translator is partly responsible for. That is the general nature of this quite specific trust' (Pym 2012, p. 76, italics original). Keeping that in mind, Pym recommends that '[i]f the translator cannot or does not want to fulfil expectations, the divergence has to be stated. You cannot cheat or trick the reader or the client. Such is the basis of what could be called an ethics of confession: we do not really care what you do, as long as you tell us about it' (2012, p. 96). This seems sensible, but not all clients would be happy with that (for instance, they might not want to pay the translator). On the other hand, an editor or publisher or other client might actually accept or even encourage a 'divergence', which would then imply that they have a duty to push the 'ethics of confession' to the next level and to tell the final reader of the product. This is something I have rarely seen. The only example I can think of was in a translation to Norwegian of Mark Twain's *The Adventures of Huckleberry Finn*. Twain's novels employ a variety of different dialects, which translator Olav Angell felt unwilling or unable to translate (see Epstein 2012, p. 222). He added an explanatory note, 'This richness of nuance is of course difficult to express in Norwegian. It would take ages to get something similar. I didn't have that much time. Mea culpa' (2003, p. 12, my translation). An ethics of confession seems to have influenced his choice to write that note.

To sum up this section, Kroger and Crots argue for the need for more research into

> actual ethical decision-making, leading to the choice of particular strategies for the translation of contentious material; motivations for particular translation choices; awareness of codified ethical guidelines; perception of their own agency in intercultural exchange in a world characterised by imbalances in power, and perception of the interaction between personal and professional ethics in their decision-making processes. (Kruger and Crots 2014, pp. 149–50)

This would be very important to analyse, but for now, translators could work on considering these points and trying to tease out how they themselves are impacted in their translation work by their own professional and personal ethics.

6.4 Stories from Translators

While it is fascinating to see how ideas of ethics have shifted over time and across situations and also where the emphasis tends to be placed in regard to responsibilities and values, I would like to return to explore how ethics, particularly the more personal ones, impact our work on a daily basis. That is to say, how do translators' own values and beliefs affect the way they work? Bennett does look at a few case studies, but in the context of how they fit with codes of conduct; for example, one could question whether pro-bono work is 'socially engaged' and thus ethical (2021, p. 45), or whether perhaps it is unethical to expect translators to work for free (i.e. to exploit them) and to potentially undervalue their work and to make it challenging for some translators to support themselves and their families. Bennett argues that 'real-life examples of ethical situations and the solutions arrived at by translators' should be included in 'commentaries accompanying translator codes' (2021, p. 46). This would be a hugely beneficial thing to include more often in translation classes and publications on translation.

In my own conversations with students, I have often heard someone say that they would or would not translate a given text or text type. The reasons they have given tended to have to do with personal ethics rather than professional ethics. As I was especially interested to know how translators think about ethics in their work, I posed a question about it in one of the many social media groups I am in that focuses on translation. This was a rather unscientific approach to the topic since I did not apply for ethical approval from a research board or use a regularly accepted methodology to analyse the results of my call for stories; I do not believe this makes my discussion of ethics unethical in and of itself, but I want to point out that this was only a casual inquiry and not a major scientific study. I made sure that the people who received my question knew this was the case and I confirmed with them that I could quote them anonymously in this book.

Reading through the many examples I received, it struck me that there were a few main categories to ethics, at least in my informal, limited study: (a) sometimes people turned down work because it chafed against their own beliefs or values, (b) sometimes they refused jobs because they were worried about the impact of that text on readers/viewers, (c) sometimes they suggested revisions or just went ahead and made the changes in order to make the text more acceptable without getting the revisions approved, and (d) sometimes they felt obliged to take on a job despite vehement disagreement with the subject matter or style because they were desperate for money.

In regard to the first category, a number of people said they rejected translation jobs about political topics when they disagreed with the political standpoints; for example, a text that the translator said was in favour of the invasion of Ukraine, while the translator was against the war. Other translators said they turned down entire jobs or at least asked to leave out passages related to topics as wide-ranging as the fur industry, the arms industry, tobacco, certain religions and dated cultural and political views. Intriguingly, pornography was mentioned quite frequently, with multiple translators saying that they refused to subtitle porn films despite the significant and easy money that was sometimes offered in the field. Many years ago, a student who was the sole financial support of their family told me that they had no choice but to accept a porn translation job even though it was against their own ethics, but other translators I spoke to in the past year were more financially secure and turned down the job.

The second ethical issue occurred when a translator was concerned that the text was offensive, illegal or inappropriate. Examples included texts that featured gambling, encouraged people into shady financial deals, contained private details about real people, advertised medicines that 'cured' illnesses or ignored certain facts about history or reality. One translator shared this story

> Some investigative reporters had put together a fake corporate website with fake people (real photos, of course), contact information, etc. It was all such obvious and amateurish fakery (sloppily copied from online templates, etc.) that I had to ask them what they were doing, and they explained they were trying to entrap consultants into offering lobbying services for a fake procurement, stating their prices, etc. They wanted to create an exposé. I declined to work further on it, and told them it was highly unethical, if not illegal. They said it had been vetted by their newspaper's legal counsel. I asked a few friends for advice on what to do, blow the whistle, or what [...] but a few days later the scam was in the news. (All quotes from translators are cited anonymously and with their approval)

Several translators noted that their role could include helping to improve suspect texts, so when they received an assignment that they felt was unethical in some way, they either made changes without discussing it with the client or else entered into a conversation with the client. In terms of just going ahead and making changes, some translators shared that words could be carefully curated to enhance or remove viewpoints in a text or to make a text more inclusive. A translator said they were given a text that denied that a certain country had a colonial past, so the translator pointed out that this was inaccurate. This ended well because the client made changes and was glad not to have published something that they could have been deeply embarrassed by in the public eye. I myself worked on a text that used offensive language about a particular group of people and the author needed an explanation about why certain words were less appropriate than others; here, we were able to agree on the right vocabulary to use, which was positive as I would not have put my name to the text otherwise. On the other hand, sometimes translators deliberately do not make changes to texts; one person said, 'My normal practice [...] is to improve the prose I get to translate. In that particular case, however, I decided to reflect the intellectual calibre of the European Right with perfect accuracy, even down to their bad grammar and spelling mistakes. Garbage in, garbage out!'

If there is a non-financial imperative for taking on a text that a translator is deeply uncomfortable with and that they feel is against their ethics, a solution proffered was to donate the fee for the assignment to a charity or another organisation, ideally one that is more in line with the translator's ethics or that works to fight against whatever the issue is. An example might be to donate the money to support a refugee from that country or to a charity that promotes veganism instead of animal farming and animal testing. Another solution was to drop a given client after that particular job if they were unwilling to make changes. This requires a certain level of financial security.

One translator summed up their feelings on ethics with this comment

> To an extent, ethics are personal, I guess, and perhaps we sometimes equate our politics with our ethics, too? I am fairly center left in my politics but would have no problem translating mainstream conservative political texts, but wouldn't touch extremist texts whether left or right, but, unless the texts were advocating violence or comparable, I think that would be a political stance rather than an ethical one.

6.5 From Theory to Practice

Anthony Pym suggests that for translators, 'The fundamental ethical question is thus not "How should I translate?' but rather "Should I translate?" The answer should be understood as an acceptance or a refusal to translate now, here, for this person, in these particular conditions. Hence a simple proposition for translator ethics: translators are firstly responsible for the decision to translate' (2012, p. 103). But as he himself immediately acknowledges, translators do not always have this flexibility or power. Some simply have to take whatever work they can, in order to pay their bills. Some are in-house translators and are required to translate whatever is put in front of them. Some are in educational programmes and are given assignments that they have little control over. And so on.

But all things being equal and you have a choice, then consider carefully and choose wisely. What values matter to you and how might they impact your work as a translator? Which texts/authors do you want to translate and why? Which clients/publishers/publications are you willing to work for and why? Which translatorial strategies might you choose for which text types? Do you want your name on the final translation and would you contribute to publicising it? How might your choices (of text, approach, etc.) impact your target text or reader or influence people's perceptions of the source text, the author and the source culture? What are the costs to you, and to others, if you carry out this translation? Are you in a translators' association and what does its code suggest? Do you agree with their guidelines? How are the answers to all these questions influenced by the culture and time in which you live, by the brief you have been given by your client, by your background, by your beliefs, by any translators' associations or other groups you belong to and so on?

You translate as yourself, as someone who lives in a particular time and place and who has had experiences and feelings and thoughts that are different from everyone else's. As mentioned in the section on identity, you cannot avoid this or pretend that your own beliefs do not affect your translation work. They do. The question is: how?

Chapter 7
CONCLUSION

This book is an eclectic discussion of a handful of translation theories and their potential impact on practising literary translators. In the foregoing sections, I explored a range of theoretical ideas, mostly from literary studies or translation studies, but with clear links to other fields, such as cultural studies and philosophy. I looked at definitions; some of the large concepts in translation studies are often treated as dichotomous, namely fidelity, equivalence, distance and (in)visibility; identity; power and ethics.

Another work on translation theory could have progressed chronologically through different views or might have focused on a particular culture, issue or theorist, but the topics included here were those that happened to appeal to me at this specific point in my own life and in the life of our world. It strikes me that as we are faced with evermore urgent challenges – pandemics, climate change, wars, constrictions on particular societal groups' movements or rights – communication is incredibly important. How we engage with one another and the ideas and feelings we share could lay the foundation for fewer – or, unfortunately, additional – problems in the future. So I believe there is a strong need to think about what we are doing when we translate and to consider how our work affects us, the people around us and the planet. Personally, I try to do that when I translate – such as by choosing only to work on books I believe in, insisting on my own visibility as a translator, or talking through changes with authors/editors with an aim to be ethical in my choices – but of course I am human, and make mistakes, and am confined by my living and working conditions.

In the introduction, I wrote about the view that theory cannot be 'applied' to practice. While I am not advocating just applying any of the ideas in this book to your work or promoting allegiance to any one approach and I would stress that a translator always has to look at an individual text as a singular case, I would argue that we do not need to see theory and practice as being in opposition. They can and should inform one another and ideally practising translators would produce theories while theorists would also be translators. This is, I know, a controversial point, as you do find, for example, art historians who cannot use any medium other than words or book reviewers who review translations without themselves being translators or knowing the language the book was translated from or writing books, but it seems to me that to be able to truly understand and theorise about a field, you should have a deep knowledge of it, one that perhaps stems from practising it. Theory is a form of knowledge, and why not take advantage of as much knowledge as we can? Knowledge is always welcome and brings with it power and responsibility.

7.1 What Next?

André Lefevere sums up the idea of translation theory very simply by referring to 'the rules observed during the process of decoding and reformulation depend on the actual situation, on the function of the translation, and on who wants it made and for whom' (1999, p. 75). While some might argue that theory should stay in the academy, discussed endlessly by people who observe what translators are doing, I would suggest that practising translators need it, and also that theory needs us. As a translator myself, I acknowledge that I sometimes complacently find myself translating a particular word in a certain way without considering what it really means in a given context, or I agree to a translation before I have given enough thought to why that text needs to be translated, who the translation will serve and whether I am the right person to translate it. To be reminded of all this is one reason why I read theory. But the reverse is true too; as a scholar, I have read – and probably even written, to my embarrassment – theoretical ideas that do not seem to take account of what translators actually do and why, or that act as if translation takes place in a vacuum, separate from the rest of the world. Translation theory needs interaction with translators in order to remember what is really at stake. In short, there is a cycle of influence and interdependence here and we must speak and read one another and communicate. Translation is, as we know, all about communication.

So now it is up to you. You could develop your own philosophy or theory of translation. Decide what works best for you and why and how that will inform what you do as a translator and what strategies you employ. You could even consider writing about your ideas and sharing them with others, to inspire and challenge other theorists and translators. At the same time, continue to read theory, both from the field of translation studies and beyond, so you too can be inspired and challenged, and can keep growing and developing as a translator.

You have agency as a translator. It is important not to forget that.

BIBLIOGRAPHY

Álvarez, R. and Vidal, M. C. Á., eds. (1996). *Translation Power Subversion*. Clevedon: Multilingual Matters.

American Library Association. (2023). Top 13 Most Challenged Books of 2022. https://www.ala.org/advocacy/bbooks/frequentlychallengedbooks/top10. Accessed 11 May 2023.

Anderson, P. (2018). Founded by Daniel Hahn, the TA First Translation Prize Announces Inaugural Shortlist. *Publishing Perspectives*. https://publishingperspectives.com/2018/01/daniel-hahn-ta-first-translation-prize-inaugural-shortlist/. Accessed 26 April 2023.

Anderson, P. (2021). In London, a Call for Publishers to Name Translators on the Cover. *Publishing Perspectives*. https://publishingperspectives.com/2021/09/international-translation-day-calling-for-translators-on-the-cover/. Accessed 26 April 2023.

Anonymous. (2023). Translators' Stories. [Shared with B. J. Woodstein, with permission to include here.]

Ashcroft, B. (2001). *Post-Colonial Transformation*. London: Routledge.

Azadibougar, O. and Haddadian-Moghaddam, E. (2019). The Persian Tradition. In Y. Gambier and U. Stecconi, eds. *A World Atlas of Translation*. Amsterdam: John Benjamins Publishing Company, pp. 149–68.

Barton, P. (2021). *Fifty Sounds*. London: Fitzcarraldo Editions.

Basalamah, S. (2019). The notion of translation in the Arab world: A critical developmental perspective. In Y. Gambier and U. Stecconi, eds. *A World Atlas of Translation*. Amsterdam: John Benjamins Publishing Company, pp. 169–192.

Bassnett, S. and Trivedi, H., eds. (1999). *Post-Colonial Translation*. London: Routledge.

Ben-Ari, N. and Levin, S. (2019). Traditions of Translation in Hebrew Culture. In Y. Gambier and U. Stecconi, eds. *A World Atlas of Translation*. Amsterdam: John Benjamins Publishing Company, pp. 193–214.

Bennett, P. M. (2021). Ethics in Translation Practice: A Comparison of Professional Codes of Conduct. *Verba Hispanica*, XXIX, pp. 31–52.

Bennett, A. and Royle, N. (1960/2014). *Literature, Criticism and Theory*, fourth edition. Abingdon, UK: Routledge.

Bishop, R. S. (1990). Mirrors, Windows, and Sliding Glass Doors. *Perspectives*, 6(3).

Boase-Beier, J. (2010). Who Needs Theory? In A. Fawcett, K. L. Guadarrama García and R. Hyde Parker, eds. *Translation: Theory and Practice in Dialogue*. London: Continuum, pp. 25–38. https://scenicregional.org/wp-content/uploads/2017/08/Mirrors-Windows-and-Sliding-Glass-Doors.pdf.

Britannica editors. (2023). William Tyndale. Britannica. https://www.britannica.com/biography/William-Tyndale. Accessed 1 February 2023.

Burton, W. M. (2010). Inverting the Text: A Proposed Queer Translation Praxis. In B. J. Epstein, ed. *In Other Words: Translating Queers/Queering Translation*, 36, pp. 54–68.
Castro, O. and Ergun, E. (2018). Translation and Feminism. In J. Evans and F. Fernandez, eds. *The Routledge Handbook of Translation and Politics*. Abingdon, UK: Routledge, pp. 125–44.
Chaffee, J. (2016). 36 Metaphors for Translation. *Words without Borders*. https://wordswithoutborders.org/read/article/2016-09/36-metaphors-for-translation-jessie-chaffee/. Accessed 1 March 2023.
Chesterman, A. and Wagner, E. (2002). *Can Theory Help Translators?* Manchester: St. Jerome.
Conacher, A. (2006). Susanne de Lotbinière-Harwood: Totally Between. In A. Whitfield, ed. *Writing between the Lines*. Waterloo, ON: Wilfrid Laurier University Press, pp. 245–66.
Dharwadker, V. (1999). Ramanujan's Theory and Practice. In S. Bassnett and H. Trivedi, eds. *Post-Colonial Translation*. London: Routledge, pp. 114–40.
Dirks, N. B., ed. (1992). *Colonialism and Culture*. Ann Arbor: University of Michigan.
Epstein, B. J. (2012). *Translating Expressive Language in Children's Literature*. Bern: Peter Lang.
Epstein, B. J. (2017). Eradicalisation: Eradicating the Queer in Children's Literature. In B. J. Epstein and R. Gillett, eds. *Queer in Translation*. Abingdon, UK: Routledge, pp. 118–28.
Epstein, B. J. and Chapman, E. L., eds. (2021). *International LGBTQ+ Literature for Children and Young Adults*. London: Anthem.
Epstein, B. J. and Gillett, R., eds. (2017). *Queer in Translation*. Abingdon, UK: Routledge.
Estopace, E. (2018). Literary Translators to Share USD 10,000 Prize Pot with Authors in National Book Awards. *Slator*. https://slator.com/literary-translators-share-usd-10000-prize-pot-authors-national-book-awards/. Accessed 26 April 2023.
Faiq, S. (2000). Arabic Translation: A Glorious Past but a Meek Present. In M. G. Rose, ed. *Beyond the Western Tradition*. Binghamton, NY: Center for Research in Translation, pp. 83–98.
Fawcett, A., Guadarrama García, K. L., and Hyde Parker, R., eds. (2010). *Translation: Theory and Practice in Dialogue*. London: Continuum.
Fuertes, A. (2019). Ethics and Translation. In R. A. Valdeón and Á. Vidal, eds. *The Routledge Handbook of Spanish Translation Studies*. pp. 417–28.
Gambier, Y. and Stecconi, U., eds. (2019). *A World Atlas of Translation*. Amsterdam: John Benjamins Publishing Company.
Gentzler, E. (2001). *Contemporary Translation Theories*. Clevedon: Multilingual Matters.
Gillberg, J. (2022). Tucking på svenska [Tucking in Swedish]. *Med Andra Ord*. No. 112, pp. 13–19.
Goldberg, D. T. and Quayson, A. (2002). *Relocating Postcolonialism*. Oxford: Blackwell.
Gopinathan, G. (2000). Ancient Indian Theories of Translation. In M. G. Rose, ed. *Beyond the Western Tradition*. Binghamton, NY: Center for Research in Translation, pp. 165–73.
Grammenidis, S. and Floros, G. (2019). The Greek-Speaking Tradition. In Y. Gambier and U. Stecconi, eds. *A World Atlas of Translation*. Amsterdam: John Benjamins Publishing Company, pp. 323–40.
Greenall, A. K., Alvstad, C., Jansen, H. and Taivalkoski-Shilov, K. (2019). Introduction: Voice, Ethics and Translation. *Perspectives*, 27(5), pp. 639–47, DOI: 10.1080/0907676X.2019.1631862.

Halme-Berneking, R. (2019). Translation Traditions in Angola. In Y. Gambier and U. Stecconi, eds. *A World Atlas of Translation*. Amsterdam: John Benjamins Publishing Company, pp. 271–86.
Hatim, B. and Munday, J. (2004). *Translation: An Advanced Resource Book*. London: Routledge.
Hermans, T. (2018). Schleiermacher. In J. P. Rawling and P. Wilson, eds. *The Routledge Handbook of Translation and Philosophy*. London: Routledge. https://discovery.ucl.ac.uk/id/eprint/10110835/1/Hermans_Chapter%201%20Schleiermacher%20Theo%20Hermans%20Final%20Version.pdf.
Inghilleri, M. and Maier, C. (1998/2011). Ethics. In M. Baker and G. Saldanha, eds. *The Routledge Encylopedia of Translation Studies*, second edition. London: Routledge.
Jakobson, R. (1959/2004). On Linguistic Aspects of Translation. In L. Venuti, ed. *The Translation Studies Reader*, second edition. London: Routledge, pp. 138–43.
Kothari, R. and Shah, K. (2019). More or Less Translation: Landscapes of Language and Communication in India. In Y. Gambier and U. Stecconi, eds. *A World Atlas of Translation*. Amsterdam: John Benjamins Publishing Company, pp. 125–48.
Kruger, H. and Crots, E. (2014). Professional and Personal Ethics in Translation: A Survey of South African Translators Strategies and Motivations. *Stellenbosch Papers in Linguistics*, 23, pp. 147–81.
Landers, C. E. (2001). *Literary Translation: A Practical Guide*. Clevedon: Multilingual Matters.
Lefevere, A. (1999). Composing the Other. In S. Bassnett and H. Trivedi, eds. *Post-Colonial Translation*. London: Routledge, pp. 75–94.
Maier, C. (1998). Issues in the Practice of Translating Women's Fiction. *Bulletin of Hispanic Studies*, 75(1), pp. 95–108.
Malmkjær, K. and Windle, K., eds. (2011). *The Oxford Handbook of Translation Studies*. Oxford: Oxford University Press.
Marais, K. (2021). Eleven Different Names, One Practice: Towards a Phenomenology of Translation. *Perspectives*, 29(3), pp. 311–25. DOI: 10.1080/0907676X.2020.1726419.
Munday, J. (2001/2008). *Introducing Translation Studies*, second edition. London: Routledge.
Nabokov, V. (1941). The Art of Translation. The New Republic. https://newrepublic.com/article/62610/the-art-translation.
Nida, E. (1964/2004). Principles of Correspondence. In L. Venuti, ed. *The Translation Studies Reader*, second edition. New York: Routledge, pp. 153–67.
Nikolajeva, M. (2010). *Power, Voice and Subjectivity in Literature for Young Readers*. London: Routledge.
Nord, C. (1997). *Translating as a Purposeful Activity: Functionalist Approaches Explained*. Manchester: St. Jerome.
Nord, C. (2007). Function plus Loyalty: Ethics in Professional Translation. *Génesis. Revista Científica do ISAG*, 6, pp. 7–17. /https://www.ufs.ac.za/docs/librariesprovider20/linguistics-and-language-practice-documents/all-documents/nord-2007function-loyalty-937-eng.pdf.
O'Brien, E. (2001–2002). Seamus Heaney and the Ethics of Translation. *Canadian Journal of Irish Studies*, 27:2–28:1, pp. 20–37.
Oittinen, R. (1993). *I Am Me – I Am Other. On the Dialogics of Translating for Children*. Tampere, Finland: University of Tampere.
Oittinen, R. (2000). *Translating for Children*. New York: Garland.
Ordóñez López, P. and Agost, R. (2022). Future Translators' Views on Translation Theory: A Qualitative Approach. *The Interpreter and Translator Trainer*, 16(2), pp. 158–76.

O'Sullivan, E. (2005). *Comparative Children's Literature.* Translated by Anthea Bell. London: Routledge.
Oxford English Dictionary. (n.d.). Faithful. https://www.oed.com/view/Entry/67763?redirectedFrom=faithful#eid. Accessed 25 April 2023.
Oxford English Dictionary. (n.d.). Literary Theory. https://www-oed-com.uea.idm.oclc.org/view/Entry/109067#eid225819960. Accessed 16 March 2023.
Oxford English Dictionary. (n.d.). Loyal. https://www.oed.com/view/Entry/110751?redirectedFrom=loyal#eid. Accessed 25 April 2023.
Oxford English Dictionary. (n.d.). Theory. https://www-oed-com.uea.idm.oclc.org/view/Entry/200431?redirectedFrom=theory#eid. Accessed 16 March 2023.
Oxford English Dictionary. (n.d.). Translation. https://www-oed-com.uea.idm.oclc.org/view/Entry/204844?redirectedFrom=translation#eid. Accessed 10 January 2023.
Oxford English Dictionary. (n.d.). Translation Theory. https://www-oed-com.uea.idm.oclc.org/view/Entry/204844?redirectedFrom=translation+theory#eid17957085. Accessed 16 March 2023.
Palekar, S. (2017). Re-Mapping Translation. In B. J. Epstein and R. Gillett, eds. *Queer in Translation.* Abingdon, UK: Routledge, pp. 8–24.
Polizzotti, M. (2018). *Sympathy for the Traitor.* Cambridge, MA: MIT Press.
Pym, A. (2009). *Exploring Translation Theories.* London: Routledge.
Pym, A. (2012). *On Translator Ethics.* Translated by Heike Walker. Amsterdam: John Benjamins.
Reynolds, P. (2005). *Ish.* London: Walker.
Robinson, D. (1997). *Translation and Empire: Postcolonial Theories Explained.* Manchester: St. Jerome Publishing.
Robinson, D., ed. (1997/2002). *Western Translation Theory from Herodotus to Nietzsche.* Manchester: St. Jerome.
Rose, M. G., ed. (2000). *Beyond the Western Tradition.* Binghamton, NY: Center for Research in Translation.
Savage, D. (2021). *Savage Love from A to Z.* Seattle: Sasquatch books.
Schleiermacher, F. (1813/2004). On the Different Methods of Translating. In L. Venuti, ed. *The Translation Studies Reader,* second edition. New York: Routledge, pp. 43–63.
Schwimmer, M. (2017). Beyond Theory and Practice: Towards an Ethics of Translation. *Ethics and Education,* 12(1), pp. 51–61.
Shavit, Z. (2006). Translation of Children's Literature. In G. Lathey, ed. The Translation of Children's Literature. Clevedon: Multilingual Matters, pp. 25–40.
Simon, S. (1996). *Gender in Translation: Cultural Identity and the Politics of Transmission.* Abingdon, UK: Routledge.
Singer, P. (2022). Ethics. *Encylopaedia Britannica.* https://www.britannica.com/topic/ethics-philosophy. Accessed 1 February 2023.
Society of Authors. (2021). #TranslatorsOnTheCover. https://www2.societyofauthors.org/translators-on-the-cover/#add-name. Accessed 26 April 2023.
St. André, J. (2011). Metaphors for Translation. In L. van Doorslaer and Y. Gambier, eds. *The Handbook of Translation Studies,* pp. 84–87. https://benjamins.com/online/hts/articles/met1. Accessed 1 March 2023.
Stewart, S. (2021). Translators Fight for Credit on Their Own Book Covers. *Publishers Weekly.* https://www.publishersweekly.com/pw/by-topic/industry-news/publisher-news/article/87649-translators-fight-for-credit-on-their-own-book-covers.html. Accessed 26 April 2023.

Szirtes, G. (2009). A Faithful Translation. https://georgeszirtes.blogspot.com/2009/09/faithful-translation.html. Accessed 12 January 2023.
TranslateDay. (2021). Faithfulness in Translation. https://www.translateday.com/faithfulness-in-translation/#:~:text=Faithfulness%20in%20translation%20defines%20how,original%20as%20it%20can%20be. Accessed 25 April 2023.
Twain, M. (2003). *Huckleberry Finn*. Translated by Olav Angell. Oslo: Kagge Forlag.
Tymoczko, M. (1999). Post-Colonial Writing and Literary Translation. In S. Bassnett and H. Trivedi, eds. *Post-Colonial Translation*. London: Routledge, pp. 19–40.
Tymoczko, M. & Gentzler, E., eds. (2003). *Translation and Power*. Amherst and Boston: University of Massachusetts Press.
UNICEF. (n.d.). The United Nations Convention on the Rights of the Child. www.unicef.org.uk/what-we-do/un-convention-child-rights/.
Venuti, L. (1995/2008). *The Translator's Invisibility*. New York: Routledge.
Venuti, L. ed. (2000/2004). *The Translation Studies Reader*, second edition. Abingdon, UK: Routledge.
von Flotow, L. (1991). Feminist Translation: Contexts, Practices and Theories. *TTR*, 4(2), pp. 69–84.
von Flotow, L. (1997). *Translation and Gender: Translation in the Era of Feminism*. Manchester: St. Jerome.
von Flotow, L. ed. (2011). *Translating Women*. Ottawa: University of Ottawa Press.
Wakabayashi, J. (2000). A Japanese Perspective on the Universalism vs Particularism Debate. In M. G. Rose, ed. *Beyond the Western Tradition*. Binghamton, NY: Center for Research in Translation, pp. 259–71.
Wakabayashi, J. (2011). Secular Translation: Asian Perspectives. In K. Malmkjær and K. Windle, eds. The Oxford Handbook of Translation Studies. Oxford: Oxford University Press, pp. 23–36.
Wallmach, K. (2006). Feminist Translation Strategies: Different or Derived? *Journal of Literary Studies*, 22(1–2), pp. 1–26.
Wilson, A. (2009). *Translators on Translating*. Vancouver: CCSP Press.
Woodstein, B. J. (2022). *Translation and Genre*. Cambridge: Cambridge University Press.
Young, R. J. C. (2006). Writing Back, in Translation. In R. J. Granqvist, ed. *Writing Back in/and Translation*. Frankfurt am Main: Peter Lang, pp. 19–38.

www.ingramcontent.com/pod-product-compliance
Lightning Source LLC
Chambersburg PA
CBHW030143170426
43199CB00008B/186